GENA
KNOX

Southern
My Way

FOOD & FAMILY

GENA
KNOX

Southern My Way

FOOD & FAMILY

GENA KNOX

PHOTOGRAPHY BY BRIAN WOODCOCK

Published in the United States by Gena Knox Media, LLC, Athens, Georgia.
www.genaknox.com

Library of Congress Control Number: 2013912279

ISBN 978-0-615-83641-6

Printed in China

Designed by Gill Autrey for Gena Knox Media, LLC

First Edition

*To Mama Chess,
my sweet grandmother and caramel cake queen*

GENA
KNOX

Contents

Peach Orchard
MIDDLE GEORGIA

Hardman Farm
SAUTEE NACOOCHEE

Introduction

ALTHOUGH MY SIBLINGS AND I WERE RAISED in the sleepy town of Reynolds, Georgia, rural life kept us so busy that I can't recall ever being bored. Any given summer afternoon, my brother Pate and I would hop on his three-wheeler and zip down our half-mile driveway, through the hay fields, across Highway 96 and onto the dirt road. We drove straight through the Wainwrights' peach orchards and down to Suggs Mill Pond to fish for bream in the spillway. I was a tiny little thing, but managed to keep up with my brother and learn how to bait my own hook.

Before we headed home, weighed down by a bucket of flopping fish, Pate and I would walk along the edges of the dirt road and pick as many blackberries as we could reach. We endured untold numbers of scratches and bug bites for the promise of a steaming cobbler we couldn't wait to dig into. Besides her wonderful way with a pail of berries, our mom could fry fresh-caught fish, whip up hushpuppies and make a batch of cheese grits blindfolded, all talents I aspired to have.

Cypress Pond
WILLMAR PLANTATION

Year after year, the twin threads of food and family wove our days together. Looking back, I'm amazed at how my mom was able to get three kids out the door for church and still have a big Sunday lunch for us when we got home, with her incredible fried chicken as the star. In summer, she liked to round out the meal with fried green tomatoes or okra and a platter of sliced ripe tomatoes. She would put my sister and me to work setting the table, shucking corn, making sour cream rolls — any tasks she needed help with.

My Grandmama Peggy lived close by in Butler, and she came over to spend almost every Sunday with us. In the afternoons, she'd sit for hours on our back porch, shelling field peas until the sun went down and sipping on a Coors Light. Thanks to her, we always had a freezer full of those tender morsels, plus a stockpile of butterbeans and corn, to enjoy throughout the winter.

When I turned 16, my dad bought a farm about an hour south of Reynolds, near Americus. He turned it into his dream: a plantation where he and our friends and family could carry on the Southern tradition of quail hunting. Now, 20 years later, Willmar Plantation has given us countless memories of family meals, quail hunts, horseback riding and even the odd snakebite. Neely, my four-year-old, loves running around the farm, playing in the barn and "shootin' birds" with his cap gun.

My husband, Davis, grew up with similarly deep-rooted traditions. From an early age, he spent summers in the Sautee Nacoochee Valley in north Georgia. Since our kids were born, we've enjoyed magical weekends on his family property with them. Neely loves to play in Dukes Creek and romp through the fields with our two Boykin spaniels. He camps with his daddy in an old cabin on the creek, while the girls stay up at the main house with running water and nice beds.

I cherish every one of our family traditions, from Sunday lunches to Christmas quail hunts, and I want nothing more than to pass them on to my own children. It's hard to believe that, years later, I have two little ones and a third on the way, and so many wonderful things to teach them.

Neely is already learning how to make biscuits and cookies, and he's become a professional biscuit dough eater, just like I was at his age. He knows how to collect eggs from our chicken coop and is fascinated by watching vegetables grow in the garden. Genevieve, my two-year-old, and the baby to be will soon follow in his footsteps. I can't tell you how much I'm looking forward to creating beautiful memories and traditions with our family of five.

Gena Knox

Starters

- Fresh Fig Flatbread
- Roasted Beet Dip
- Crabby Hushpuppies
- Homemade Buttermilk Crackers
- Oven-Roasted Summer Tomatoes
- Oven-Roasted Tomato and Goat Cheese Crostini
- Olive Cream Cheese Spread
- Baked Marinated Feta
- Smoked Trout Blinis
- Georgia Shrimp Ceviche
- White Cheddar-Wrapped Pecans
- Fried Green Tomatoes
- Apple Cider Bellini
- Edamame and Avocado Spread
- Peter Piper's Pepper Jelly

Bloodroot Blades
SEE RESOURCES, PAGE 232

Fresh Fig Flatbread
with Country Ham and Blue Cheese

If anyone asks me what my favorite food is, my answer is figs. I have two trees in
my yard and I know the location of every fig tree in our neighborhood. Next to fig preserves,
which I eat every morning, this recipe is my favorite way to use them. You can serve it
as a starter or pair it with a salad to make a meal for four.

PREP TIME 25 minutes plus 1 hour to rise
COOK TIME 12 minutes
YIELDS 12 servings

Dough

¾ cup warm water
1 package RapidRise Yeast
2 cups all-purpose or bread flour
1 teaspoon sugar
¾ teaspoon kosher salt
3½ tablespoons olive oil, divided
Cornmeal for dusting

Toppings

8 to 12 fresh figs, cut in half or in quarters
    depending on size
2 ounces thinly sliced country ham or
    prosciutto
2 ounces good-quality blue cheese
1½ tablespoons honey
1½ cups baby arugula
Olive oil for serving

FIRST Stir yeast into warm water and set aside to dissolve, about 5 minutes. In a food processor, combine flour, sugar and salt. Coat a large mixing bowl with ½ tablespoon oil and set aside. Once yeast has dissolved, stir 3 tablespoons olive oil into yeast mixture. With motor running, slowly pour yeast mixture into flour until a sticky ball forms (you may not use all the liquid).

NEXT Place dough inside mixing bowl, toss to coat with oil and cover with plastic wrap. Set in a warm, draft-free place and let rise about 1 hour or until doubled in size. Preheat oven to 425°F. Punch dough down and place on a floured work surface. Sprinkle lightly with flour and knead with hands until dough is no longer sticky, about 20 seconds. Divide dough in half and, using a rolling pin, roll each half into a 7x14-inch rectangle.

LAST Sprinkle two baking sheets lightly with cornmeal to prevent sticking. Transfer one dough rectangle to each sheet. Bake until edges are lightly browned, about 8 minutes. Arrange ham over; top with figs and blue cheese. Drizzle lightly with olive oil and return to oven for 3 to 4 minutes or until cheese melts. Drizzle with honey, top with arugula and serve.

FROM MY KITCHEN Short on time? Purchase fresh pizza dough at your local grocery store, and this recipe takes just 10 minutes to prep.

Roasted Beet Dip
with Crumbled Feta

I absolutely love beets, and this dip is so easy and delicious.
Sprinkled with salty feta and paired with warm flatbread or crisp crudités,
it will quickly become one of your favorites too.

PREP TIME 15 minutes
COOK TIME 45 minutes
YIELDS 1 cup

3   medium beets, greens trimmed,
     bottom ½ inch of stems left intact
1   small garlic clove, minced
½   cup plain nonfat or 2 percent Greek yogurt
1½ tablespoons olive oil, plus more for finishing
⅛   teaspoon ground cumin, toasted
     (see From My Kitchen, below)
Pinch ground coriander
2   teaspoons fresh lemon juice
1   tablespoon crumbled feta cheese
1   tablespoon chopped fresh parsley or
     chives for garnish
Warm flatbread, pitas or vegetables for serving

FIRST Preheat oven to 350°F. Wrap each beet separately in aluminum foil; place on roasting pan. Bake 45 minutes or until tender when pierced with a fork. Set aside to cool.

NEXT Peel beets by running cold water over them and sliding skins off by hand. Cut into wedges; place in food processor. Add garlic and yogurt and pulse until blended. With processor running, slowly drizzle in olive oil and process until smooth. Transfer puree to a medium bowl and stir in cumin, coriander, lemon juice and salt to taste.

LAST Top puree with crumbled feta, parsley and olive oil. Serve with warm flatbread, pitas or fresh vegetables.

FROM MY KITCHEN Toasting spices enriches their flavor. Heat cumin in a small, dry skillet over medium-low heat, stirring often, until fragrant, about 15 seconds.

Crabby Hushpuppies

Hushpuppies are my weakness (really, who doesn't love them?).
When I was a kid, we always had them with fried catfish, and now I occasionally
make them for a fun treat. I dress mine up with fresh crab and a tangy Southern dipping sauce,
but you can swap in Vidalia onions and fresh corn if you like.

PREP TIME 15 minutes
COOK TIME 15 minutes
YIELDS About 20

Comeback Sauce

½ cup light or regular mayonnaise
2 tablespoons ketchup
2 tablespoons chili sauce
1 teaspoon Dijon mustard
¼ teaspoon garlic powder
1 teaspoon Worcestershire sauce
¼ cup olive oil
Juice of ½ lemon
Tabasco sauce to taste

Hushpuppies

¾ cup yellow cornmeal
½ cup all-purpose flour
1½ teaspoons baking powder
1 teaspoon sugar
1 teaspoon garlic powder
¾ teaspoon kosher salt
½ teaspoon baking soda
½ teaspoon cayenne pepper
¾ cup buttermilk
2 large eggs, lightly beaten
½ pound fresh crabmeat, tiny shells removed
¼ cup finely chopped scallions
1½ quarts canola oil for cooking
Lemon wedges and Comeback Sauce to serve

FIRST Combine sauce ingredients in a small bowl and refrigerate until ready to serve.

NEXT In a large bowl, combine cornmeal, flour, baking powder, sugar, garlic, salt, baking soda and cayenne. Whisk in buttermilk and eggs. Stir in crab and scallions. Allow batter to rest at least 10 minutes.

LAST Pour a 3-inch depth of canola oil into a large Dutch oven. Heat over medium-high heat (oil is ready when a pinch of flour sizzles, or thermometer inserted in oil reaches 350°F). Drop batter into oil by heaping tablespoons; cook about 1½ minutes per side or until golden brown. Remove hushpuppies and place on baking sheet lined with newspaper to drain. Serve with lemon wedges and Comeback Sauce. Store leftover hushpuppies in refrigerator and reheat in a 425°F oven.

Homemade Buttermilk Crackers

I always feel extra proud stocking the pantry with crackers made from scratch,
not out of a box. Take them from simple snack to sophisticated appetizer by serving them with
fresh goat cheese or Brie and Peter Piper's Pepper Jelly (page 43).

PREP TIME 30 minutes plus 1 hour chill time
COOK TIME 20 minutes
YIELDS About 65 crackers

1½ cups all-purpose flour, plus more
    for sprinkling
1½ cups whole-wheat flour
1½ tablespoons sugar
1 teaspoon baking powder
½ teaspoon kosher salt, plus more for topping
1½ cups buttermilk, divided
⅓ cup olive oil, plus more for brushing
5 tablespoons sesame seeds

FIRST In a medium bowl, whisk together all-purpose flour, whole-wheat flour, sugar, baking powder and ½ teaspoon salt. Make a well in center of mixture; pour in 1 cup buttermilk and olive oil. Slowly whisk to incorporate flour into the liquid until dough forms. Add an additional ½ cup buttermilk if dough appears too dry. Sprinkle a work surface lightly with flour and knead dough for about 30 seconds. Shape into a rectangle, wrap with plastic wrap and refrigerate for 1 hour.

NEXT Preheat oven to 350°F. Line 2 to 3 rimmed baking sheets with parchment paper. Cut dough into thirds and place one third on floured surface; refrigerate remaining dough. Roll into a rectangle the thickness of a quarter. Using both hands, transfer dough to baking sheet. Brush with olive oil and sprinkle with sesame seeds and kosher salt, pressing seeds gently into dough to stick. Using a sharp knife or pizza cutter, cut dough lengthwise into 2-inch-wide strips. Cut each strip into 3-inch-long pieces and trim any uneven edges. Spread crackers on baking sheets, leaving a little space between each cracker.

LAST Bake crackers until lightly browned and crisp, about 20 minutes. Repeat with remaining dough. Store crackers in an airtight container at room temperature.

Oven-Roasted Summer Tomatoes

This is one recipe every summer gardener or farmer's market shopper should have on hand. What better way to preserve fresh, ripe tomatoes than slow roasting, which concentrates the delicious flavors? I freeze the roasted tomatoes, then thaw them as needed to use for pastas and sauces, to pair with cheese for appetizers, or to stuff in avocado sandwiches.

PREP TIME 20 minutes
COOK TIME 2 to 3 hours
YIELDS About 24 tomato halves

4½ pounds medium fresh tomatoes (about 12)
Sugar
Kosher salt
1 tablespoon balsamic vinegar
3 cloves garlic, thinly sliced
1 tablespoon fresh thyme
¼ cup olive oil

FIRST Adjust oven rack to middle position and preheat oven to 350°F. Line two rimmed baking sheets with foil and top with parchment paper. Remove stems from tomatoes and cut in half horizontally. Arrange, cut sides up, on baking sheet.

NEXT Sprinkle each tomato with a pinch of sugar and salt. Drizzle with balsamic; top with garlic. Sprinkle thyme leaves over and drizzle with olive oil. Move tomatoes around slightly to coat bottoms in oil as well.

LAST Roast tomatoes until they are half their original height and the edges are deep brown, about 2 to 3 hours depending on size. Layer tomatoes between sheets of parchment paper in a freezer-safe container. Freeze; thaw as needed.

FROM MY KITCHEN If you're using Roma tomatoes, cut them in half from stem to tip. Roast for about 2 hours.

Oven-Roasted Tomato and Goat Cheese Crostini

In college, my roommate Caroline and I would spend much of our time in the kitchen cooking and drinking wine. When she paired honey with tomatoes I thought she was crazy, but the combination, amped up with goat cheese and fresh mint, turned out to be spectacular.

PREP TIME 15 minutes
COOK TIME 8 minutes
Yields 12 crostini

12 (½-inch-thick) diagonally cut baguette slices
1 tablespoon olive oil
6 ounces goat cheese, room temperature
6 oven-roasted tomato halves (page 25)
Honey to drizzle
2 tablespoons fresh mint, coarsely chopped

FIRST Preheat oven to 350°F. Arrange baguette slices on a baking sheet and brush each lightly with olive oil. Bake until lightly browned, about 7 to 8 minutes.

LAST Cut tomatoes in half. Spread crostini with goat cheese and top with tomato halves. Arrange crostini on a platter and lightly drizzle with honey. Top with mint, season to taste with freshly ground black pepper and serve.

Olive Cream Cheese Spread

This delicacy was one of the most popular hors d'oeuvres my mom and
her catering partner served at weddings. My Grandmama Peggy and I spent many
Friday afternoons smoothing the mixture onto small bread rounds and packing them up
for the next day. I always looked forward to the leftover spread for sandwiches.

PREP TIME 10 minutes
YIELDS 1½ cups

1   cup pimento-filled green olives, drained
8   ounces light cream cheese, softened
1   tablespoon Greek yogurt
Paprika to garnish

FIRST Using a food processor or blender, finely chop olives and set aside.

NEXT Fold cream cheese and yogurt into olives.

LAST Sprinkle a pinch of paprika over mixture and serve.

> **FROM MY KITCHEN** Serve this delicious spread with a platter of fresh vegetables for dipping. Or follow my mom's example and cut sandwich bread into rounds with a small biscuit cutter, then spread the olive mixture on top and garnish with paprika.

Baked Marinated Feta

Dinner party guests go wild for this starter, and it takes no time to prepare.
South Carolina's Split Creek Farm crafts a delicious feta that's hard to resist.
If you can find a local version in your area, though, all the better.

PREP TIME 5 minutes plus 30 minutes
marinating time
COOK TIME 10 minutes
YIELDS 6 servings

1 (6-ounce) block feta cheese,
cut into ½-inch-thick slices
¼ cup olive oil
1 tablespoon chopped fresh basil
2 teaspoons fresh thyme leaves
Zest of ½ lemon
⅛ teaspoon fennel seeds, crushed
⅛ teaspoon red pepper flakes
Fresh bread for serving

FIRST Preheat oven to 400°F. Arrange feta slices in a small baking or gratin dish. Top with olive oil, basil, thyme, zest, fennel and red pepper.

NEXT Turn feta to coat completely with oil and seasonings. Let marinate at room temperature for 30 minutes, flipping after 15 minutes.

LAST Bake until slightly bubbly and beginning to brown, about 10 minutes. Serve warm with fresh bread.

Smoked Trout Blinis
with Chives and Crème Fraîche

Keep these little savory pancakes in your freezer for last-minute guests.
You can top them with anything, but the flavor of smoked trout,
combined with the silkiness of crème fraîche, is a standout.

PREP TIME 15 minutes
COOK TIME 10 minutes
YIELDS About 35 blinis

Blinis

2 eggs, lightly beaten
½ cup sour cream
¼ cup all-purpose flour
¼ teaspoon salt
⅛ teaspoon baking soda
1 tablespoon finely chopped chives
Canola oil for coating pan

Topping

Crème fraîche, about ½ cup
4 to 6 ounces smoked trout
Cayenne pepper
Chopped chives or microgreens for garnish

FIRST Whisk eggs and sour cream together and set aside. In a medium bowl, whisk flour, salt and baking soda. Spoon dry ingredients into egg mixture and whisk until smooth. Fold in chives.

NEXT Heat a 12-inch skillet over medium heat. Coat skillet with 1 teaspoon canola oil and wipe down with a paper towel. Working in batches, spoon batter into skillet by ½ tablespoons to form 1 ½-inch to 2-inch rounds. Cook until bubbles appear on surface and undersides are golden brown, about 1 minute. Flip and cook an additional minute or until brown. Transfer to a serving platter; repeat with remaining batter.

LAST Top each blini with a dollop of crème fraîche and ½-inch chunk of smoked trout. Sprinkle with cayenne pepper and chopped chives or microgreens to serve.

> **FROM MY KITCHEN** If your local market doesn't carry crème fraîche, you can easily substitute sour cream or make your own. To do so, combine 1 cup whipping cream with 2 tablespoons buttermilk. Cover and let sit at room temperature for 10 to 24 hours until thickened. Refrigerate up to 2 weeks.

Georgia Shrimp Ceviche
with Saltine Crackers

If you're lucky enough to come across fresh, local shrimp, you must try this recipe.
My parents live in St. Simons, Georgia, now, and my mom always
keeps my freezer stocked with shrimp from the area. They really put this dish
over the top. It is perfect as a starter, but in the unlikely event you have leftovers,
they're wonderful on top of a salad. Saltines are a must for serving.

PREP TIME 15 minutes plus 1 hour chill time
COOK TIME 10 minutes
YIELDS About 35 blinis

1   pound small, local shrimp
    (about 40 per pound), unpeeled
2   teaspoons salt
¼   cup fresh lime juice
½   cup finely chopped tomato
¼   cup roughly chopped cilantro
¼   cup sliced green olives with pimentos
2   tablespoons finely chopped red onion
1 to 2 tablespoons finely chopped fresh jalapeno
2   tablespoons fresh orange juice
2   tablespoons olive oil
1   medium avocado, peeled, pitted and diced
Saltine crackers to serve

FIRST Heat 1 quart cold water, shrimp and salt in a saucepan over medium-high heat. After shrimp turn pink (about 7 minutes), drain in a colander and cover with ice to cool.

LAST Peel shrimp and place in a medium bowl. Toss with lime juice and refrigerate for 30 minutes. Stir in tomato, cilantro, olives, onion, jalapeno, orange juice and oil. Season to taste with additional salt and freshly ground black pepper; chill at least 30 minutes. Just before serving, fold in avocado. Serve with saltines.

White Cheddar-Wrapped Pecans

There is no telling how many of these savory morsels my mom has
made in her catering career — way too many to count. They've always flown
right off the silver serving trays as fast as she can replenish them.
They freeze well and make great snacks for last-minute guests.

PREP TIME 20 minutes
COOK TIME 15 minutes
YIELDS About 45

1   (10-ounce) block sharp white cheddar,
    room temperature
1   stick (½ cup) unsalted butter, softened
1½ cups all-purpose flour
1   teaspoon kosher salt
½   teaspoon cayenne pepper or more to taste
About 45 pecan halves

FIRST Preheat oven to 350°F. Grate cheese using a food processor or hand grater. Combine shredded cheese, butter, flour, salt and pepper in a food processor fitted with blade attachment. Process until dough forms a ball and separates from side of processor.

NEXT Using hands, roll dough into 1-inch balls and place on ungreased baking sheet, about 2 inches apart. Place 1 pecan half in center of each ball and press gently so that pecan is embedded in dough.

LAST Bake for 15 minutes until lightly browned. Allow to cool before serving.

Fried Green Tomatoes
with Peach Salsa

My mom always had a garden full of tomatoes, but it seems like we rarely let them
get ripe — fried green tomatoes were a staple at our summer Sunday lunches. Her secret is a dash
of hot sauce on top of each slice before breading and frying. When testing this recipe, I managed
to convert two fried green tomato skeptics into big fans. That's always a good sign!

PREP TIME 15 minutes
COOK TIME 20 minutes
YIELDS 4 to 6 servings

Peach Salsa

2   cups fresh peaches, peeled, pitted and
     chopped (about 3 peaches)
1   avocado, peeled, pitted and diced
2   tablespoons finely diced red onion
Juice of ½ lime

Fried Green Tomatoes

4   medium green tomatoes
¾   cup white cornmeal
½   cup all-purpose flour
¾   teaspoon kosher salt
1   egg, lightly beaten
2   tablespoons water
1½ cups canola oil
Hot sauce (such as Tabasco)

FIRST Combine peaches, avocado, onion and lime juice.
Season with a pinch of salt and set aside. Slice tomatoes
into ½-inch slices; set aside.

NEXT Preheat oven to 225°F. In a 9-inch pie plate, combine
cornmeal, flour and salt; season with freshly ground black
pepper. In a separate bowl, whisk together egg and water.
Heat oil in a 12-inch cast-iron skillet. Dredge each tomato
slice in egg mixture and lay in flour mixture. Top each
tomato slice with 2 to 3 drops of hot sauce; dredge in flour
mixture to coat. Fry tomatoes in batches for 3 to 4 minutes
per side or until golden brown. Drain on a baking sheet
lined with paper towels.

LAST Transfer tomatoes to a wire cooling rack set over a
rimmed baking sheet and place in oven to keep warm, if
desired. Serve on a platter with Peach Salsa on the side.

Apple Cider Bellini

I love sparkling wine more than any other cocktail.
I remember sipping Welch's sparkling grape juice on New Year's Eve as a small child,
thinking I was so special. This twist on a Bellini is a delicious party starter throughout
the fall — serve it to your Thanksgiving guests for an extra touch of elegance.

PREP TIME 5 minutes
COOK TIME 10 minutes
YIELDS About 10 servings

1½ cups fresh apple cider
⅛ teaspoon ground cinnamon
⅛ teaspoon ground cardamom
4 whole cloves
¼ teaspoon freshly grated nutmeg
2 bottles chilled Prosecco or cava

FIRST Bring apple cider to a boil in a saucepan over medium-high heat. Simmer until reduced by half, about 12 minutes. Stir in cinnamon, cardamom, cloves and nutmeg; set aside to cool.

LAST Strain cider through a fine-mesh strainer, discarding leftover spices. Pour 4 teaspoons cider mixture into each glass, top with sparkling wine and serve.

Edamame and Avocado Spread

This spread has become our stand-in for hummus. My kids love it, it's good for them and it's also easy to make. I like to slather it on whole-grain bread and top it with sliced tomato, cucumber and sprouts for a last-minute lunch.

PREP TIME 10 minutes
YIELDS 2½ cups

1   (12-ounce) package frozen shelled edamame, thawed (about 2½ cups)
1   avocado, peeled, pitted and diced
1   small shallot, roughly chopped
Zest and juice of 1 lemon
      (about 3 tablespoons juice)
½   teaspoon ground cumin
¼   teaspoon ground coriander
½   teaspoon kosher salt
2   tablespoons olive oil
2   tablespoons water
2   tablespoons chopped fresh parsley

FIRST In a food processor, combine edamame, avocado, shallot, lemon zest and juice, cumin, coriander and salt. Pulse until almost smooth. Scrape down sides using a rubber spatula. Add oil, water and parsley; process until smooth. Season with freshly ground black pepper, if desired.

LAST Serve with crudités or crackers, or as a sandwich spread.

Peter Piper's Pepper Jelly

Our good friend Peter, known for his brownies (page 197), also makes
a mean pepper jelly that I put on everything from grilled cheese to pork tenderloin.
It pairs especially well with Brie and goat cheese for a simple starter or snack.

PICTURED ON PAGE 23

PREP TIME 20 minutes
COOK TIME 12 minutes
YIELDS 6 half-pint jars

2   red bell peppers, stems and veins removed,
    roughly chopped
8   jalapeno peppers, stems and seeds removed,
    1 tablespoon seeds reserved
5   cups sugar
1½ cups apple cider vinegar
2   (3-ounce) pouches liquid pectin

Special equipment:
    Rubber or plastic gloves
    Cheesecloth
    6 half-pint canning jars, sterilized

FIRST Place bell peppers in a food processor fitted with metal blade attachment and pulse until finely chopped but not pureed. Measure out exactly two cups, reserving remaining peppers for another use. Place jalapenos in processor and pulse until finely chopped; measure jalapenos to equal 1½ cups. Discard remaining jalapenos.

NEXT Wearing gloves, place peppers in center of a double layer of cheesecloth, gather ends together and twist to wring out any excess liquid. (Make sure peppers are thoroughly dry for ideal results.) In a 5-quart pot over medium-high heat, combine peppers, reserved jalapeno seeds, sugar and vinegar. Stir until sugar is dissolved. Increase heat to high and bring to a boil, allowing mixture to boil 3 minutes. Remove from heat and let cool 5 minutes.

LAST Add pectin and stir about 3 minutes, making sure peppers are distributed evenly. Carefully ladle hot jelly into canning jars. Secure lids and let cool. The heat of the jelly should properly seal lids. As the jars cool, turn lids to secure tightly.

Soups

- Carrot Ginger Soup
- Spring Vegetable, Chicken and Orzo Soup
- Baby Turnip and Potato Soup
- Summer Soup
- Chilled Cucumber Soup
- Sweet Potato Soufflé Soup
- Smoky Split Pea Soup
- Chilled Peach Soup (pictured)

Carrot Ginger Soup

I know I've found a winning recipe when my four-year-old asks for seconds!
Coconut milk adds luxurious richness to one of my favorite flavor combinations: carrots and
fresh ginger. Top the soup with pepitas or toasted pumpkin seeds for a nice crunch.

PREP TIME 15 minutes
COOK TIME 25 minutes
YIELDS 6 servings

2   teaspoons olive oil
½   medium sweet onion, chopped (about 1 cup)
3   cloves garlic, chopped
1   pound carrots, roughly chopped
1   small potato (6 ounces), peeled
2   teaspoons grated fresh ginger
3½ cups low-sodium chicken stock
1   teaspoon salt
1½ cups light coconut milk
2   teaspoons lemon juice
Cayenne, cilantro and pepitas to garnish

FIRST Heat oil in a large stockpot over medium-high heat. Sauté onion and garlic until soft, about 5 minutes. Stir in carrots, potato and ginger; sauté an additional minute. Add stock and bring to a boil. Reduce heat to a simmer; cover and cook 20 minutes or until carrots are tender.

LAST Puree soup with a soup emulsifier or, working in batches, in a blender (take care to avoid burns). Stir in coconut milk and lemon juice; season with freshly ground black pepper. Ladle into bowls and garnish with cayenne, cilantro and pepitas.

Spring Vegetable, Chicken and Orzo Soup

Early spring in the South is unpredictable. Just when spireas and azaleas bloom and we are gearing up for the Masters Golf Tournament, a cold snap will hit. This soup is full of spring color and flavors, but it's comforting and warm on a cool, damp day.

PREP TIME 15 minutes
COOK TIME 25 minutes
YIELDS 4 to 6 servings

1 tablespoon olive oil
1 medium Vidalia onion, chopped
   (about 2 cups)
2 carrots, sliced ¼ inch thick (about 1 cup)
1 celery rib, sliced ¼ inch thick
2 sprigs fresh thyme
½ cup white wine
6 cups homemade or store-bought
   low-sodium chicken stock
2 egg yolks
3 tablespoons fresh lemon juice, divided
2 cups poached or roasted chicken, shredded
   (see From My Kitchen, below)
¾ cup uncooked orzo pasta
¼ pound asparagus, cut into 1-inch pieces
   (1 cup)
½ cup fresh or frozen green peas
1 tablespoon tarragon, finely chopped
½ teaspoon fresh lemon zest

FIRST Heat oil in a large stockpot over medium heat. Add onion, carrots and celery and sauté until tender, stirring often, about 5 minutes. Add thyme and wine and cook about 1 minute. Stir in stock and bring to a boil.

NEXT While stock comes to a boil, whisk egg yolks and 2 tablespoons lemon juice in a small bowl. Ladle ½ cup of hot stock mixture into yolks, whisking constantly. Slowly whisk warmed egg mixture into soup. Reduce heat and simmer 10 minutes. Stir in chicken and orzo and cook until pasta is al dente, about 5 minutes.

LAST Add asparagus and peas and continue cooking until asparagus is bright green, about 1 more minute. Stir in remaining 1 tablespoon lemon juice, tarragon and zest. Season with salt and freshly ground black pepper to taste.

FROM MY KITCHEN For the best flavor, roast bone-in, skin-on chicken breasts, seasoned with salt, pepper and olive oil, at 350°F. Once chicken cools, remove skin and shred by hand.

Baby Turnip and Potato Soup

As a child, I was never a fan of turnips. If I walked in the door from school and smelled that distinctive odor, I'd turn around immediately, dreading dinner. When I was introduced to baby turnips as an adult, though, they changed my mind. Their mild flavor is just right for this creamy soup, delicious on a brisk fall day.

PREP TIME 20 minutes
COOK TIME 22 minutes
YIELDS 4 to 6 servings

1 tablespoon olive oil
1 sweet onion, chopped (about 1 cup)
1 pound baby turnips, stems removed, halved
1 pound Yukon Gold potatoes, peeled, cut into 1-inch pieces
3 cups low-sodium chicken stock
1 teaspoon kosher salt
¼ cup finely grated fresh Parmesan, plus more for garnish
1 tablespoon chopped chives
Olive oil to finish

FIRST Heat oil in a large stockpot over medium-high heat. Sauté onion until translucent but not brown, about 5 minutes. Add turnips and potatoes and cook, stirring often, an additional 2 minutes. Add stock and salt; bring to a simmer and cook 15 minutes or until turnips and potatoes are tender.

NEXT Allow soup to cool slightly. Using a soup emulsifier or working in batches in a blender or food processor, puree until smooth. Return to pot and stir in cheese. Season to taste with salt and freshly ground black pepper.

LAST Ladle soup into bowls. Top with Parmesan and chives, drizzle with olive oil and serve.

> **FROM MY KITCHEN** If you're weighing turnips with stems on, they should equal about 2 pounds. If baby turnips are not available, use regular turnips, but peel them and dice into 1-inch pieces.

Summer Soup

One of my longtime favorite restaurants is Portofino in Atlanta. They serve a similar version of this summer soup (or, for old-school Southerners, "summa" soup) that I never stop craving. Use only ripe, really good summer tomatoes for the best results.

PREP TIME 20 minutes plus 1 hour chill time
COOK TIME 10 minutes
YIELDS 6 servings

Soup

2 pounds tomatoes, cored and roughly chopped
2 celery ribs, roughly chopped
½ English cucumber, roughly chopped
1 red bell pepper, stem and core removed, roughly chopped
¼ cup chopped flat-leaf parsley
¼ cup chopped fresh basil
½ cup water
¼ cup extra-virgin olive oil
3 tablespoons sherry vinegar
1 tablespoon sugar
½ tablespoon kosher salt
Juice of ½ lime

Croutons

2 cups rustic bread, cut into ½-inch pieces
1 tablespoon olive oil

FIRST Preheat oven to 375°F. Working in batches in a blender or food processor, puree tomatoes, celery, cucumber, bell pepper, parsley and basil until almost smooth or to desired consistency. Transfer to a large bowl and stir in water, oil, vinegar, sugar, salt and lime juice. Season to taste with freshly ground black pepper.

NEXT Chill soup for at least an hour before serving. While soup chills, toss bread cubes with oil and spread in an even layer on a rimmed baking sheet. Bake, tossing occasionally, until golden, about 10 minutes.

LAST Ladle soup into bowls, top with croutons and serve.

Chilled Cucumber Soup

Susan Mason is one of the most amazing women I know. A longtime caterer in Savannah, Georgia, she is renowned for her Southern cuisine, grace and hospitality. Her Chilled Cucumber Soup is a must for hot Low Country days.

PREP TIME 10 minutes
COOK TIME 40 minutes
YIELDS 4 regular servings or 6 small

Soup

- 1 tablespoon olive oil
- 5 cucumbers, peeled, seeded and chopped
- 1 leek, white part only, thinly sliced and washed
- 1 bay leaf
- 1 tablespoon flour
- 3 cups low-sodium chicken stock
- 1 teaspoon salt
- 1 cup 1 percent milk
- ½ cup Greek yogurt
- Juice of ½ lemon

Garnish

Chopped fresh mint
1   cucumber, peeled, seeded and chopped
Greek yogurt

FIRST Heat oil in a Dutch oven over medium heat. Sauté cucumber, leek and bay leaf until vegetables are soft, about 15 minutes. Remove bay leaf and whisk in flour to thicken. Add stock and salt. Bring to a boil, reduce heat and simmer 25 minutes.

NEXT Using a soup emulsifier or working in batches in a blender, puree soup until smooth. Press soup through a fine-mesh sieve using a rubber spatula; discard solids. Chill in refrigerator or, if short on time, in a metal mixing bowl set over a large bowl of ice. Stir occasionally until cool.

LAST Stir in milk; whisk in yogurt and lemon juice. Season to taste with salt and freshly ground black pepper. Serve with mint, chopped cucumber and yogurt on the side.

Sweet Potato Soufflé Soup

In our house, the holidays wouldn't be the same without sweet potato casserole, my favorite side dish. I converted it into a quick-cooking soup that I make throughout the fall and winter. My children absolutely love it!

PREP TIME 10 minutes
COOK TIME 35 minutes
YIELDS 6 servings

Soup

3   medium sweet potatoes
    (about 2 ½ pounds), peeled and diced
2   teaspoons olive oil
1   medium onion, chopped
5   cups low-sodium chicken stock, divided
3   tablespoons brown sugar
¾   teaspoon salt
1¼ teaspoons ground cinnamon
¼   teaspoon ground nutmeg
2   teaspoons grated fresh ginger
½   tablespoon butter

Toppings

Mini marshmallows
Toasted pecans

FIRST Fill a large stockpot with salted water and bring to a boil. Cook potatoes until fork-tender, about 15 minutes. Drain and set aside.

NEXT Heat oil in a large pot and sauté onion until lightly browned and tender, about 7 minutes. Add potatoes, 4 cups stock, brown sugar, salt, cinnamon and nutmeg; simmer 15 minutes. Using a handheld soup emulsifier, blend soup until smooth. (If you don't have an emulsifier, puree soup in several batches using a blender, taking care to avoid burns.) Stir in ginger and butter; season to taste with salt and freshly ground black pepper. If soup is too thick, add extra stock to reach desired consistency.

LAST Ladle soup into bowls. Top with mini marshmallows and pecans to serve.

Smoky Split Pea Soup

During the cooler months, I rely on easy soups for lunch. This hearty, flavorful soup is super-healthy and freezes perfectly. I often top a big bowl of it with toasted crostini and creamy goat cheese for a little crunch.

PREP TIME 10 minutes
COOK TIME 40 minutes
YIELDS 6 servings

1   tablespoon olive oil
1   carrot, chopped
1   onion, chopped
1   stalk celery, chopped
1   pound dried split peas, rinsed and drained
6   cups low-sodium chicken stock
2   cups water
½   teaspoon dried thyme
1½ teaspoons salt
½   cup oil-packed sun-dried tomatoes, drained
½   teaspoon smoked paprika

FIRST Heat oil over medium heat in a large Dutch oven or stockpot. Sauté carrots, onions and celery until soft, about 6 minutes. Add peas, stock, water, thyme and salt; bring to a boil. Reduce heat to low, cover and simmer about 35 minutes or until peas are tender. Stir in sun-dried tomatoes.

LAST Using a handheld emulsion blender, food processor or blender, puree soup until smooth and creamy. Stir in paprika. Season to taste with salt and freshly ground black pepper and serve.

Chilled Peach Soup

During summer in the South, we have ways of incorporating peaches into every course. This soup is so refreshing in the Georgia heat. You can serve it as a light lunch or even as a little something sweet at the end of a meal.

PICTURED ON PAGES 44-45

PREP TIME 10 minutes plus 1 hour chill time
COOK TIME 10 minutes
YIELDS 4 cups

4   cups fresh peach slices (from about
    5 medium peaches, peeled)
1   cup dry white wine (such as Pinot Grigio)
1   (3-inch) cinnamon stick
⅛   teaspoon ground cardamom
2   tablespoons honey
Juice of ½ lemon
6   ounces plain yogurt, plus extra for thickening
¼   teaspoon vanilla extract
Fresh mint for garnish

FIRST In a medium saucepan, combine peaches, wine, cinnamon and cardamom over medium-high heat. Bring to a boil; reduce heat, cover and simmer 10 minutes or until peaches are soft.

NEXT Remove peaches from heat and let cool slightly. Remove and discard cinnamon stick. Puree in food processor or blender until smooth. Add honey, lemon juice, yogurt and vanilla; pulse until smooth. Thicken with additional yogurt if needed.

LAST Refrigerate soup until chilled, at least 1 hour. Ladle into bowls, garnish with fresh mint and serve.

Salads

- Spring Salad
- Glazed Acorn Squash and Arugula Salad
- Bibb Wedge Salad
- Mixed Greens
- Peach and Tomato Salad
- Buttermilk Caesar Salad
- Hearts of Palm Salad
- Kale and Avocado Salad
- Roasted Pear and Spinach Salad

Spring Salad

with Creamy Lemon Dressing

My husband built wonderful raised planters for our home in Athens, Georgia. Every spring and fall, I plant more lettuce and arugula than I can shake a stick at. They taste so much better than their store-bought counterparts, and this simple dressing makes their flavors pop. If you don't garden, just pick up an assortment of greens at your local farmers' market.

PREP TIME 10 minutes
YIELDS 6 servings

Dressing

Zest and juice of 1 lemon
½ cup light sour cream
1 tablespoon finely chopped shallot
1 teaspoon Dijon mustard
½ cup olive oil

Salad

½ pound assorted spring lettuces such as Bibb, Red Oak and romaine (about 12 cups total)
1 cup thinly sliced radishes
1 avocado, peeled, pitted and diced

FIRST In a small bowl, combine zest, juice, sour cream, shallot, mustard and olive oil until smooth. Season with salt and freshly ground black pepper to taste; set aside.

LAST Arrange greens on salad plates or platter. Top with radishes and avocado; drizzle with dressing.

Glazed Acorn Squash and Arugula Salad
with Apple Cider Maple Dressing

This salad, which I serve almost every week throughout the fall and winter, is one of my favorite ways to celebrate the bounty of the harvest season. Tangy goat cheese and dried cranberries strike just the right contrast with sweet, caramelized squash. Sometimes I simply roast the squash and serve it as a side dish.

PREP TIME 20 minutes
COOK TIME 35 minutes
YIELDS 6 servings

Squash

2 acorn squash, halved through stems, seeded
1 tablespoon olive oil
2 teaspoons brown sugar
½ teaspoon kosher salt
3 tablespoons pure maple syrup
½ tablespoon butter, melted
Pinch cayenne pepper

Dressing

1½ tablespoons apple cider vinegar
½ tablespoon pure maple or cane syrup
½ teaspoon Dijon mustard
2 tablespoons olive oil

Salad

5 ounces baby arugula
2 ounces goat cheese
½ cup dried cranberries

FIRST Preheat oven to 475°F. Slice squash halves into 1½-inch rings and toss in a large bowl with oil, sugar and salt. Arrange squash in a single layer on a greased baking sheet and roast in oven until bottom sides are nicely browned, about 20 to 25 minutes. Combine maple syrup, butter and cayenne in a small bowl and set aside.

NEXT Meanwhile, whisk dressing ingredients in a small bowl and season to taste with salt and freshly ground black pepper; set aside. When bottoms of squash slices are browned, flip and brush maple syrup mixture over them. Return to oven and cook until golden, about 12 minutes.

LAST Toss arugula in a large bowl with desired amount of dressing. Arrange on a serving platter or salad plates. Top with roasted squash and sprinkle with goat cheese and dried cranberries.

Bibb Wedge Salad
with Blue Cheese Yogurt Dressing

This dressing, which highlights my updated version of a traditional wedge salad,
is so much healthier than many of its creamy cousins. The Bibb lettuce makes
a beautiful presentation, just right for serving family-style.

PREP TIME 10 minutes
YIELDS 4 servings

Dressing

½ cup low-fat Greek yogurt
1 small garlic clove, finely minced
2 tablespoons white wine vinegar
2 tablespoons fresh lemon juice
2 tablespoons water
¼ cup crumbled blue cheese

Salad

1 head Bibb lettuce, outer leaves removed
2 strips bacon, cooked and crumbled
2 eggs, soft-boiled

FIRST In a small bowl, combine yogurt, garlic, vinegar, lemon juice and water. Stir in blue cheese and season to taste with salt and freshly ground pepper. Set aside.

LAST Cut head of lettuce in half, then cut each half in quarters, stem to tip. Arrange on a platter, drizzle with dressing and sprinkle with bacon. Arrange eggs alongside salad and top with freshly ground black pepper to serve.

Mixed Greens

with Fresh Cherries and Shallot Thyme Vinaigrette

I eat my fair share of cherries when they come into season in early summer.
Many folks don't think of using them in dishes other than cobblers or pies, but they're
amazing in salads and pair well with goat cheese or blue cheese, whichever you like.

PREP TIME 10 minutes
YIELDS 4 servings

Dressing

2 tablespoons Champagne vinegar or white wine vinegar
1 tablespoon finely chopped shallots
1 teaspoon fresh thyme, chopped
½ teaspoon honey
3 tablespoons olive oil

Salad

3 ounces mixed greens (about 7 cups)
1 cup fresh cherries, pitted and halved
2 ounces fresh goat cheese
¼ cup pecan halves, lightly toasted

FIRST In a small bowl, whisk together vinegar, shallots, thyme, honey and olive oil. Season with salt and freshly ground black pepper.

LAST Toss greens and cherries with dressing. Divide among 4 plates and top with goat cheese and pecans to serve.

Peach and Tomato Salad

As long as you have good summer tomatoes and fresh peaches,
you cannot go wrong with this salad. Most people don't realize that peaches and
tomatoes work beautifully together, especially when they gain a little edge from salty feta.
I serve this with grilled salmon or halibut when I entertain, and it always goes over well.

PREP TIME 15 minutes plus 20 minutes
  marinating time
YIELDS 4 servings

Dressing

2 tablespoons finely chopped shallots
1½ tablespoons Champagne vinegar
½ teaspoon sugar
¼ teaspoon kosher salt
2 tablespoons olive oil

Salad

2 cups assorted cherry tomatoes, halved
2 cups sliced fresh peaches
2 ounces feta, broken into large chunks
¼ cup fresh basil, roughly chopped

FIRST In a small bowl, combine shallots, vinegar, sugar
and salt. Whisk in olive oil, season to taste with freshly ground
black pepper and set aside.

LAST Place tomatoes, peaches and feta in a large bowl.
Gently toss with dressing and allow to marinate at room
temperature for 20 minutes. Fold in basil and serve.

Buttermilk Caesar Salad

Everyone loves a classic Caesar salad. Instead of the heavy, creamy dressing
most of us are used to, though, I like to substitute this version, which gets
a nice tanginess from the buttermilk. Plus, it's actually good for you!

PREP TIME 10 minutes
COOK TIME 10 minutes
YIELDS 6 servings

Dressing

½ cup low-fat buttermilk
¼ cup light mayonnaise
1½ tablespoons lemon juice
1 teaspoon Worcestershire sauce
1 garlic clove, minced
¼ cup finely grated fresh Parmesan cheese

Salad

2 cups rustic bread, torn into 1-inch pieces
2 tablespoons olive oil
3 romaine lettuce hearts
Parmesan cheese curls to top

FIRST Preheat oven to 375°F. In a medium bowl, whisk buttermilk, mayonnaise, lemon juice, Worcestershire and garlic. Stir in cheese; season to taste with salt and freshly ground black pepper.

NEXT Toss bread with olive oil and arrange in a single layer on a baking sheet. Toast in oven, tossing occasionally, until crisp and lightly browned, about 10 minutes.

LAST Strip whole leaves from romaine hearts and place in a large salad bowl. Using hands, toss with croutons and enough dressing to taste. Arrange on salad plates and top with Parmesan cheese curls.

FROM MY KITCHEN Parmesan cheese curls sound fancy, but they couldn't be easier to create. Just run a vegetable peeler along a block of cheese, and the shavings will curl right off.

Hearts of Palm Salad

with Tangerines and Avocado

Right out of college, I worked as a landscape architect for Georgia's beautiful Sea Island Resort.
Any time a palm tree had to come down, the crew would strip off the outer leaves,
remove the heart and pass it around for us to snack on. Of course, I don't recommend
harvesting your own hearts of palm — just buy them at your local market.
Add crumbled blue cheese to make this refreshing salad a little richer.

PREP TIME 10 minutes
YIELDS 6 servings

Dressing

1   tablespoon rice wine vinegar
1   teaspoon tangerine zest
1   tablespoon tangerine juice
2   tablespoons olive oil
1   teaspoon Dijon mustard
2   tablespoons finely chopped shallots

Salad

6   cups trimmed arugula
4   tangerines or 2 navel oranges, peeled and
    cut into ¼-inch slices
1   (14-ounce) can or jar hearts of palm,
    drained and cut into ½-inch slices
1   avocado, peeled, pitted and thinly sliced
6   radishes, thinly sliced (optional)

FIRST In a small bowl, whisk together vinegar, zest, juice, oil, mustard and shallots. Season to taste with salt and freshly ground black pepper; set aside.

LAST In a large bowl, toss arugula with desired amount of dressing. Add tangerines, hearts of palm, avocado and radishes, if using. Toss gently and serve.

Kale and Avocado Salad
with Lemon Vinaigrette

I love all hearty greens, from kale to collards to mustard greens. I must say,
that was not always the case — as a kid, I dreaded the smell of greens cooking on our stove.
Now, though, this is one of my favorite salads, and the simple flavors of lemon and olive oil are
so refreshing. It's always better made ahead, and leftovers are delicious for lunch.

PREP TIME 15 minutes plus 1 hour
   marinating time
YIELDS 4 servings

Dressing

2 tablespoons fresh lemon juice
Zest of ½ lemon
1 teaspoon Dijon mustard
¾ teaspoon kosher salt
½ teaspoon sugar
¼ cup olive oil

Salad

1 bunch kale, center stems removed,
   thinly sliced crosswise (about 8 cups)
½ cup finely shredded fresh Parmesan cheese
1 avocado, peeled, pitted and diced
1 cup cherry tomatoes, halved
2 tablespoons pine nuts, lightly toasted

FIRST In a small bowl, combine lemon juice, zest, mustard,
salt, sugar and olive oil. Toss dressing with kale and cheese.
Let marinate in refrigerator for at least 1 hour or overnight.

LAST Just before serving, toss with avocado, tomatoes
and pine nuts.

Roasted Pear and Spinach Salad

I love warm salads throughout the fall and winter months, and roasted pears add an extra layer of richness to this one. Topped with blue cheese, it goes nicely with wild game dinners, or even a classic Thanksgiving meal.

PREP TIME 10 minutes
COOK TIME 15 minutes
YIELDS 4 servings

Salad

2   pears, cored, each cut into 8 wedges
2   teaspoons melted butter
½   tablespoon brown sugar
6   cups fresh baby spinach
¼   cup toasted pecans
2   ounces blue cheese, thinly sliced
4   pitted Medjool dates, sliced

Dressing

2   tablespoons balsamic vinegar
3½ tablespoons olive oil
1   teaspoon Dijon mustard

FIRST Preheat oven to 400°F. Toss pears with butter and sugar and arrange in a single layer on baking sheet lined with parchment. Roast until tender, about 10 to 15 minutes.

LAST In a small bowl, whisk together vinegar, oil and mustard; season to taste with salt and freshly ground black pepper. Toss spinach with desired amount of dressing. Arrange on platter or divide among 4 salad plates. Top with roasted pears, pecans, blue cheese and dates to serve.

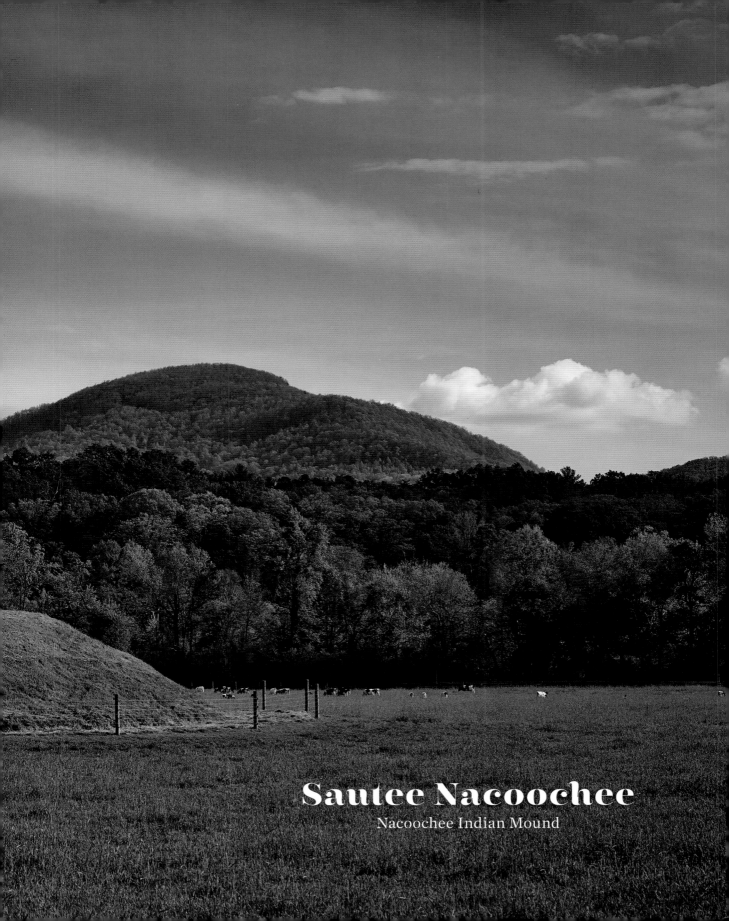

Sautee Nacoochee

Nacoochee Indian Mound

Gena and Genevieve
SAUTEE NACOOCHEE

Hardman Farm
SAUTEE NACOOCHEE

Lunch

- Farro Salad
- Mediterranean Tuna Salad
- Waldorf Chicken Salad
- German Potato Salad
- Broccoli Salad
- Tomato and Goat Cheese Tart
- The Ultimate Turkey Burger
- Homemade Mayonnaise
- Shrimp Salad (pictured)
- Fruit Salad (pictured)

Farro Salad

with Mango, Cucumber and Mint

Farro has become one of my new favorite ingredients — it is healthy, delicious and so versatile. You can use it in dishes from risotto to cool summer salads like this one, which I often eat for weekday lunches. I usually stir in the avocado right before serving so it doesn't get mushy.

PREP TIME 15 minutes
COOK TIME 30 minutes
YIELDS 8 to 10 servings

3   teaspoons salt, divided
2   cups farro, rinsed and drained
3   tablespoons olive oil
Juice of 1 lime (about 2 tablespoons)
Zest of ½ lime
1   tablespoon rice wine vinegar
1   mango, peeled, cut into small cubes
1   cup chopped English cucumber
¼   cup chopped flat-leaf parsley
¼   cup chopped fresh mint
2   ounces feta cheese, crumbled (about ½ cup)
2   cups shredded roast chicken or
    fresh cooked shrimp (optional)
2   avocados, peeled, pitted and diced
    (about 2 cups)

FIRST In a large stockpot, bring 3 quarts of water and 2 teaspoons salt to a boil. Add farro; reduce heat to a low boil. Cook until farro is tender but still has a bite, about 30 minutes. Drain and place in a large mixing bowl to cool slightly.

LAST In a small bowl, whisk oil, lime juice, zest, vinegar and 1 teaspoon salt. Toss with farro. Stir in mango, cucumber, herbs and feta. Fold in chicken or shrimp, if using, and avocado. Serve chilled or at room temperature.

Mediterranean Tuna Salad

My mom and my best friend Anne's mom, Mrs. Jane, were catering partners. I can remember when Anne and I "invented" our first fancy hors d'oeuvre, which we ate almost every summer day for lunch: tuna salad with mayo and dill pickle stuffed inside Bugle chips (the cone-shaped chips many of us grew up with). My recipe for tuna salad has come a long way — I love this lighter version with a simple vinaigrette, tucked inside pitas instead of cheese-flavored Bugles.

PREP TIME 15 minutes
YIELDS 6 servings

Dressing

Juice and zest of 1 lemon
1   tablespoon Dijon mustard
3   tablespoons olive oil

Salad

24 ounces solid white albacore tuna packed in
     water, drained
¾   cup thinly sliced celery
¼   cup finely chopped red onion
¼   cup Kalamata olives, pitted and
     finely chopped
2   ounces feta cheese, crumbled (⅔ cup)
2   tablespoons fresh oregano, finely chopped

FIRST In a small bowl, whisk juice, zest, mustard and olive oil.

NEXT Place tuna in a large mixing bowl; fold in celery, onion, olives, feta and oregano. Drizzle with dressing and toss to coat. Season with salt and freshly ground black pepper to taste.

LAST Serve immediately or refrigerate.

Waldorf Chicken Salad

Mrs. Jane, who taught me almost as much about cooking as my mom,
introduced me to this dish when I was young. It's not exactly a true Southern classic,
but it's full of great memories for me.

PREP TIME 20 minutes plus chill time
COOK TIME 35 minutes
YIELDS 8 servings

½ cup raisins
¼ cup fresh orange juice
3 bone-in, skin-on chicken breasts
1 apple, cored and cubed
2 teaspoons fresh lemon juice
½ cup plus 2 tablespoons nonfat Greek yogurt
   (about 6 ounces)
¼ cup light or regular mayonnaise
1 tablespoon Dijon mustard
1 teaspoon orange zest
1 cup thinly sliced celery
½ cup toasted, chopped pecans
2 large handfuls arugula

FIRST Preheat oven to 350°F. Place raisins and orange juice in a small bowl; set aside. Drizzle chicken with olive oil and season with salt and freshly ground black pepper. Roast on a baking sheet lined with parchment paper until meat thermometer inserted in thickest part of breast registers 165°F, about 35 minutes. Remove from oven and cool. With your hands, shred enough chicken to yield 4 cups.

NEXT Toss cubed apple with lemon juice; set aside. In a large mixing bowl, combine yogurt, mayonnaise, mustard and zest. Fold in chicken; season to taste with salt and freshly ground black pepper.

LAST Stir in raisins and juice, celery and pecans; chill until ready to serve. Just before serving, gently fold in arugula.

German Potato Salad

Growing up, I cringed at the sight of mayonnaise-laden potato salad, so my mom often made her version of German potato salad instead. It's still one of my favorites today, and it's particularly nice with grilled summer fare.

PREP TIME 20 minutes
COOK TIME 15 minutes
YIELDS 10 servings

Salad

3 pounds small red-skinned potatoes
1 cup chopped celery
½ cup thinly sliced scallions (about 6)
3 hard-boiled eggs, halved lengthwise and thinly sliced
3 strips cooked bacon, crumbled

Dressing

5 tablespoons olive oil
3 tablespoons red wine vinegar
1½ teaspoons salt
¼ teaspoon sugar

FIRST Cut potatoes into halves or quarters, depending on size, and place in a large stockpot. Fill pot with cold water and season generously with salt. Bring to a boil; reduce heat and simmer until potatoes are tender when pierced with a knife, about 15 minutes. Drain and set aside.

LAST While potatoes are cooking, combine oil, vinegar, salt and sugar in a small bowl and set aside. Place potatoes in a large mixing bowl. Gently toss with dressing and season with freshly ground black pepper. Fold in celery, scallions, eggs and bacon. Serve slightly warm or at room temperature.

Broccoli Salad

with Orange Yogurt Dressing

At Sunday church lunches in my hometown, mayonnaise-coated broccoli salad always
had a place on the buffet table — usually next to the green marshmallow dish that someone called
"salad." I far prefer this version, with a hint of fresh orange and a light yogurt dressing.
Pack it as a picnic side or an easy lunch on the go.

PREP TIME 15 minutes
COOK TIME 6 minutes
YIELDS 4 servings

Dressing

5 tablespoons Greek yogurt
2 tablespoons fresh orange juice
2 teaspoons orange zest
2 teaspoons rice wine vinegar
1 tablespoon honey
1 tablespoon canola oil

Salad

2 pounds broccoli
1 teaspoon kosher salt
½ cup thinly sliced celery
¼ cup dried cranberries
¼ cup chopped walnuts, toasted

FIRST Combine yogurt, orange juice, zest, vinegar and
honey in a small bowl. Whisk in oil. Season to taste with salt
and freshly ground black pepper; set aside.

NEXT Cut broccoli into small florets, trimming off and
discarding woody parts of stalks. Using a vegetable peeler,
peel the outer ⅛ inch from each stalk. Cut stalks in half
lengthwise, then into bite-size pieces. You should have
about 9 cups broccoli. Fill a large stockpot with about 2 inches
of water and add salt. Bring to a simmer. Add broccoli, replace
lid and steam for about 6 minutes, tossing once, or until
broccoli is crisp-tender. While broccoli is cooking, prepare a
large bowl of ice water. Using tongs, plunge cooked broccoli
into ice water to cool. Drain and set aside.

LAST Transfer broccoli to a large mixing bowl. Add celery
and cranberries and toss with enough dressing to coat.
Sprinkle with walnuts. Serve immediately or refrigerate
until ready to eat.

Tomato and Goat Cheese Tart

When tomatoes and basil are at their peak in the summer, I manage to incorporate them into almost every meal I eat. I love serving this as a starter or pairing it with chicken salad for a warm-weather lunch.

PREP TIME 20 minutes
COOK TIME 35 minutes
YIELDS 6 servings

Cornmeal Crust

⅔ cup all-purpose flour
⅔ cup yellow cornmeal
¼ teaspoon kosher salt
2½ tablespoons unsalted butter, cut into slices
2 tablespoons canola oil
5 tablespoons ice water

Filling

4 ounces goat cheese, softened
1¼ pounds fresh tomatoes, assorted sizes
   and colors
1 teaspoon olive oil, plus more for serving
¼ cup fresh basil leaves

FIRST Preheat oven to 400°F. In a food processor fitted with blade attachment, pulse flour, cornmeal and salt together. Add butter and oil; pulse until mixture resembles coarse meal. With processor on, slowly add ice water until mixture forms a loose dough (do not allow a ball to form). You might not use all of the water.

NEXT Press dough into the bottom and up the sides of a 9-inch tart pan with detachable rim. Bake for 20 minutes or until crust just starts to brown. Spread goat cheese in an even layer on warm crust. Slice tomatoes ¼ inch thick; arrange slices in an overlapping pattern on crust. Sprinkle with kosher salt and freshly ground black pepper to taste. Drizzle 1 teaspoon olive oil over.

LAST Bake tart for 15 minutes, remove from oven and top with basil leaves. Drizzle with additional oil just before serving.

The Ultimate Turkey Burger

I cooked my first turkey burger in college, and it tasted like cardboard.
Determined to make these burgers as rich and delicious as their beef counterparts,
I've had fun over the years experimenting with all kinds of ingredients. This version is
loaded with flavor and smokiness and gets a little punch from
unexpected ingredients such as peach preserves.

PREP TIME 10 minutes plus 30 minutes
chill time
COOK TIME 15 minutes
YIELDS 6 servings

Sauce

¼ cup peach preserves
2 tablespoons Dijon mustard
4 teaspoons white wine vinegar

Burger

1 tablespoon olive oil
⅓ cup finely chopped sweet onion
½ medium Granny Smith apple,
unpeeled, diced
2 pounds lean ground turkey
1½ teaspoons kosher salt
3 teaspoons Tabasco sauce
6 ounces white cheddar or mozzarella cheese
2 avocados, peeled, pitted and thinly sliced
or mashed
Hamburger buns, arugula and good-quality
ketchup for serving

FIRST Combine preserves, mustard and vinegar in a small bowl. Season with freshly ground black pepper and set aside.

NEXT Heat oil in a medium skillet over medium heat. Sauté onion and apple until tender, about 5 minutes. Place turkey in a large mixing bowl; add onion mixture, salt, Tabasco and 2 tablespoons peach sauce. Mix gently with hands and form into 6 patties. With thumb, press an indentation in center of each patty. Refrigerate 30 minutes.

LAST Preheat grill to medium-high heat. Grill burgers for 5 minutes; flip and cook for an additional 3 minutes. Brush both sides with remaining sauce and grill for an additional minute on each side or until turkey is cooked through. Remove from heat and top with cheese; let rest 5 minutes before serving. Serve on toasted buns with avocado, arugula and ketchup.

Homemade Mayonnaise

SEE PAGES 104-105 FOR RECIPES

Homemade Mayonnaise

I don't love store-bought mayonnaise, but homemade is a different story.
I am always encouraging people to make their own mayonnaise — it is super-easy and
better for you, and the flavor is over the top. There are so many delicious ingredients
you can stir in; the possibilities to tailor it to your tastes are endless.

PREP TIME 5 minutes
YIELDS 1 cup

1   large egg yolk, room temperature
2   teaspoons lemon juice
1   teaspoon Dijon mustard
¼   teaspoon kosher salt
1   teaspoon cold water
¾   cup canola oil

FIRST In a medium bowl, whisk together egg yolk, lemon juice, mustard, salt and water until frothy.

NEXT Slowly drizzle about ¼ cup of oil into the egg mixture, whisking constantly, until mayonnaise is thick and oil is incorporated. When mayonnaise emulsifies and starts to thicken, add remaining oil in a steady, thin stream while whisking.

LAST Stir in desired flavor additions (see below) and serve immediately or refrigerate up to 3 days.

··· MAYONNAISE ADDITIONS ···

1. Caper

1   recipe Homemade Mayonnaise
1   tablespoon finely chopped capers

Serving suggestions: Brush on fish before grilling or serve on top of freshly grilled fish; serve with smoked salmon; stir into deviled eggs or tuna salad; use as a dipping sauce for steamed artichokes.

2. Smoked Paprika and Lemon

1   recipe Homemade Mayonnaise
2   teaspoons fresh lemon zest
½   teaspoon smoked paprika

Serving suggestions: Serve over grilled seafood; slather on a turkey burger; use as a sandwich spread with roast chicken, arugula and fresh tomatoes; use as a dipping sauce for grilled chicken kabobs; fold into chicken or tuna salad.

3. Roasted Garlic and Rosemary

1   recipe Homemade Mayonnaise
2   garlic cloves, peeled
1   teaspoon fresh rosemary
¼   teaspoon freshly ground black pepper

Set a small sauté pan over medium heat. Place garlic cloves in pan and roast, turning often, until slightly brown and soft, about 5 minutes. Allow garlic to cool. Using side of knife, smash cloves into a paste. Stir garlic into mayonnaise; add rosemary and black pepper.

Serving suggestions: *Spread on sandwiches (especially tomato); fold into chicken salad; place a small spoonful atop freshly grilled steak, fish or chicken. Brush onto fish or chicken before grilling; dollop on crostini, top with ripe tomato slices and serve as an appetizer; spread on your favorite burger.*

4. Ginger and Lime

1   recipe Homemade Mayonnaise
1½ teaspoons lime zest
1   teaspoon grated fresh ginger

Serving suggestions: *Brush on salmon, tuna or chicken before or after grilling; spread on a roast chicken sandwich with sliced cucumber and carrots; toss with finely chopped Napa cabbage for an easy slaw. Serve alongside grilled or boiled shrimp; spread on crostini and top with seared tuna slices and fresh cucumber; incorporate into chicken salad or tuna salad.*

5. Kalamata Olive

1 recipe Homemade Mayonnaise
1 tablespoon finely chopped Kalamata olives

Serving suggestions: *Spread on tomato sandwiches; stir into tuna salad; toss with warm pasta, toasted breadcrumbs and grilled salmon; dab on grilled fish and chicken.*

Shrimp Salad
with Roasted Red Peppers

After a long morning on the beach at our family vacation spot,
Amelia Island, Florida, my mom would always serve a big bowl of
freshly made shrimp salad. Pressed between slices of soft white sandwich bread is
still my dad's favorite way to enjoy it. I add roasted red peppers, basil and feta
to put a contemporary twist on an old Southern favorite.

PICTURED ON PAGES 86-87

PREP TIME 20 minutes plus chill time
YIELDS 6 servings

Shrimp

2 pounds small to medium fresh shrimp, unpeeled
½ lemon, thinly sliced
1 teaspoon black peppercorns
1 bay leaf
2 teaspoons salt

Salad

¼ cup light or regular mayonnaise
2 teaspoons fresh lemon juice
2 teaspoons capers
3 tablespoons chopped fresh basil
½ cup chopped roasted red peppers
½ cup thinly sliced celery
2 scallions, white and green parts, thinly sliced
2 ounces feta, crumbled (about ¼ cup)

FIRST Fill a large pot with 3 quarts cold water. Add shrimp, lemon, peppercorns, bay leaf and salt. Set over high heat and cook until shrimp are pink, stirring often, about 8 minutes. While shrimp are cooking, fill a large bowl with ice water. Once shrimp are done, drain and place into cold water to stop cooking. Drain, peel and set aside.

LAST In a large mixing bowl, combine mayonnaise, lemon juice, capers and basil. Fold in shrimp, peppers, celery, scallions and feta. Season to taste with salt and freshly ground black pepper. Chill and serve.

FROM MY KITCHEN I roast my own peppers, simply because it is so easy. Cut a red bell pepper in half lengthwise and remove seeds. Place, cut side down, on a baking sheet lined with foil. Broil until skin is blackened and blistered. Remove from oven and gather foil around peppers to trap hot steam. Let sit for 10 minutes, unwrap and cool. Skins will slide right off.

Fruit Salad

with Lime and Cayenne

My home in Reynolds was surrounded by peach orchards, but just down the road was
Mr. Albritton's huge field of watermelon. We'd load one on the back of our three-wheeler and
throw it in our pool to chill. Armed with a salt shaker and lots of paper towels,
my brother, sister and I would feast on the melon until our bellies were full.
This tumble of blackberries, peaches and watermelon, all delicious summer fruits
that thrive in the South, takes me straight back to those days.

PICTURED ON PAGES 86-87

PREP TIME 10 minutes plus chill time
YIELDS 6 to 8 servings

2 cups fresh watermelon, cut into 1-inch cubes
2 cups fresh peach slices, unpeeled
Zest of 1 lime
2 tablespoons fresh lime juice
3 teaspoons sugar
Pinch cayenne pepper (optional)
¼ cup fresh mint, chopped
3 kiwi fruit, peeled and sliced
1 cup fresh blackberries

FIRST Combine watermelon and peaches in a large mixing bowl. Gently toss with lime zest, juice, sugar and cayenne, if using.

LAST Fold in mint, kiwi and blackberries, taking care not to bruise fruit. Serve chilled.

Willmar Plantation
Bobwhite Quail Hunting

Tack Room
WILLMAR PLANTATION

Supper

- Tommy's Cornish Hens
- Sautéed Red Snapper
- My Mama's Spaghetti
- White Bean Chicken Chili
- Shrimp and Grits
- Lime Grilled Chicken
- Honey Soy-Glazed Quail
- Grilled Ribeyes
- Lemon-Roasted Fish
- Pecan Horseradish-Stuffed Trout
- Doves in Red Wine
- Rosemary-Garlic Grilled Venison Backstrap
- Maple Pecan-Glazed Chicken
- Italian Sausage and Tomato Soup
- Easy Barbecue
- Cedar-Planked Salmon
- Chicken, Artichoke and Wild Rice Casserole
- Goat Cheese Grits
- Low Country Boil (pictured)

Tommy's Cornish Hens

with Fresh Herbs

I created this recipe for my dad, who loves Cornish hens, and I have to say —
it's the most delicious chicken I've ever eaten. After a rubdown with salt and herbs and
a long rest in the fridge, the birds come out unbelievably moist and succulent.
Local Cornish hens or poussins are best, if you can get your hands on them,
but the widely available Bell & Evans brand makes a fine substitute.

PREP TIME 10 minutes plus 3 hours
    brining time
COOK TIME 45 minutes
YIELDS 4 to 8 servings, depending on
    size of birds

Dry Brine

2   tablespoons kosher salt
2   tablespoons finely chopped fresh basil
2   tablespoons finely chopped fresh rosemary
2   tablespoons finely chopped fresh oregano

4   Cornish game hens, 1¼ to 1½ pounds each
4   tablespoons balsamic vinegar
2   tablespoons olive oil

Special equipment: kitchen string (optional)

FIRST In a small bowl, combine salt and herbs; set aside. Rinse hens under cold water, pat dry and place in a glass baking dish. Rub a teaspoon of herb mixture inside the cavity of each bird. Rub remaining mixture over skin, making sure to coat breasts and thighs well. Refrigerate hens, uncovered, at least 3 hours or up to 5 hours.

NEXT Adjust oven rack to middle position and preheat oven to 400°F. Remove hens from refrigerator and let sit at room temperature while oven heats; do not rinse. In a small bowl, whisk vinegar and oil; set aside. Place a wire cooling rack over a large rimmed baking sheet lined with parchment paper. Arrange birds, breast sides down, on rack, leaving a little space in between. Tie legs together with kitchen string, if desired. Brush with some of the balsamic mixture and roast until backs begin to brown, about 25 minutes.

LAST Remove pan from oven and, using tongs, flip hens breast sides up. Brush breasts and legs with balsamic mixture. Return to oven and roast for an additional 20 to 25 minutes or until meat thermometer registers 165°F when inserted in thickest part of breast, brushing with balsamic mixture just before done. Let birds rest 10 minutes before serving.

> **FROM MY KITCHEN** I always brine chicken and pork when I have time — it makes an amazing difference in flavor and texture. Brining pulls moisture into the meat and makes it incredibly tender. For smaller birds, I prefer dry brining over wet brining, simply because I love the extra-crisp skin it yields. Plus, the cleanup is so much easier.

Sautéed Red Snapper

My dad took frequent fishing trips while I was growing up, mainly to the Apalachicola area of Florida's Gulf Coast. We were never in short supply of fresh snapper, and my mom knew the perfect way to prepare it. This simple, savory dish has become a much-requested classic for our extended family.

PREP TIME 15 minutes
COOK TIME 15 minutes
YIELDS 4 servings

Spice Blend

2   teaspoons garlic salt
2   teaspoons onion powder
1   teaspoon Spanish paprika
½   teaspoon sugar
¼   teaspoon ground turmeric
⅛   teaspoon cayenne pepper, or more to taste

1   cup panko breadcrumbs
5   tablespoons all-purpose flour
1   egg
4   (6-ounce) red snapper fillets, skin on
3   tablespoons clarified butter
    (see From My Kitchen, below)
Lemon wedges to serve

FIRST Combine spice blend ingredients in a small bowl and set aside. Combine breadcrumbs and flour in a pie plate; stir in spices and season with freshly cracked black pepper.

NEXT In a second pie plate, lightly beat egg with 3 tablespoons water. Melt butter in a 12-inch skillet (preferably cast iron) over medium heat. One piece at a time, dredge fish in egg mixture, then in flour mixture, pressing gently for coating to adhere.

LAST Sauté fish 4 minutes per side, flipping once, or until golden brown and cooked through. If your skillet is smaller, cook fish in 2 batches, using 1½ tablespoons of butter at a time. Serve with lemon wedges to squeeze over.

FROM MY KITCHEN Clarified butter (distilled of milk fat and water) has a high smoke point and works best for sautéing. Simply melt 1 stick unsalted butter on the stovetop over low heat. Remove from heat and let stand 5 minutes. Skim foam from the top and slowly pour the clear golden butter into a small bowl, leaving the milky solids in the bottom of the pan.

My Mama's Spaghetti

My mom's spaghetti is such a tradition in our family that we can both make it straight from memory. After so many of my friends begged for the recipe, I decided I had to include it in this book. The sauce is so easy — you will never purchase the jarred kind again. Freeze it in batches and you'll have a head start on weeknight family meals.

PREP TIME 10 minutes
COOK TIME 35 minutes
YIELDS 6 servings

2   teaspoons olive oil
1   cup chopped green bell pepper
1   small onion, chopped (about 1 cup)
1   pound ground bison, sirloin or turkey
3   cloves garlic
2   (14-ounce) cans diced tomatoes, preferably
    fire-roasted (such as Muir Glen)
1   (14-ounce) can tomato sauce
1½ teaspoons dried oregano or
    1 tablespoon fresh
1   bay leaf
1   teaspoon dried thyme
¼   teaspoon red pepper flakes
1   tablespoon salt
1   pound spaghetti, uncooked
2   teaspoons balsamic vinegar
¼   cup fresh basil, chopped
Freshly grated Parmesan cheese to serve

FIRST Heat oil over medium-high heat in a large Dutch oven. Sauté peppers and onions until slightly soft, about 5 minutes. Add meat, stirring to break up any clumps, and cook until no longer pink, about 5 minutes. Add garlic and cook until fragrant, about 30 seconds. Drain extra fat from pot, if desired.

NEXT Stir in tomatoes, tomato sauce, oregano, bay leaf, thyme and red pepper; simmer over low heat for 30 minutes. During the last 10 minutes of cooking, bring a large pot of water to a boil; add salt and spaghetti. Cook until al dente and drain (do not rinse).

LAST Stir vinegar and basil into sauce; season with salt to taste. Serve over spaghetti with Parmesan cheese.

White Bean Chicken Chili

In our family, we love chili, especially this one. I serve it with tortilla chips for "dipping,"
which always excites my four-year-old. The recipe makes a lot, so it's perfect for
football game get-togethers during the fall and winter.

PREP TIME 15 minutes
COOK TIME 1 hour
YIELDS 10 servings

1   strip bacon, diced
1   medium onion, chopped
3   cloves garlic, minced
2½ cups shredded cooked chicken
1   teaspoon ground cumin
1   teaspoon smoked paprika
¾   teaspoon chipotle chili powder
6   cups chicken stock
1   (28-ounce) can fire-roasted diced tomatoes
    (such as Muir Glen)
4   (15-ounce) cans Great Northern beans,
    rinsed and drained
2   (4-ounce) cans diced green chilies
1   teaspoon salt
Shredded cheese, diced avocado, cilantro and
    sour cream to top

FIRST Heat a large stockpot over medium-high heat.
Add bacon and cook until crisp. Add onion and garlic;
sauté until tender and starting to brown, about 8 to 10
minutes. Add chicken, cumin, paprika and chili powder
and cook, stirring constantly, about 2 minutes.

NEXT Add stock, tomatoes, beans, chilies and salt. Bring
to a boil, reduce heat and simmer until liquid is partially
reduced, about 45 minutes to 1 hour.

LAST Using a potato masher, mash some of the beans so
that the soup has a slightly creamy consistency. Serve with
desired toppings.

Shrimp and Grits

I don't know a soul — Southern or otherwise — who doesn't love shrimp and grits.
This version is one of my favorites because it's much lighter than most others. Grits with a kiss of
goat cheese make a spot-on match for the savory tang of capers and artichoke hearts.

PREP TIME 15 minutes
COOK TIME 20 minutes
YIELDS 4 servings

Sauce

1   strip bacon, chopped
½   medium Vidalia onion, chopped
3   cloves garlic, minced
1   red bell pepper, chopped (about 1 cup)
1   (8- to 10-ounce) package frozen artichoke
    hearts, thawed and drained
1   cup white wine
1¼ cups low-sodium chicken stock
2   teaspoons fresh thyme
1   teaspoon dried oregano or 2 teaspoons fresh
1   tablespoon all-purpose flour
1   pound fresh medium shrimp, peeled,
    tails left intact
Zest and juice of ½ lemon
¼   cup chopped fresh parsley
1½ tablespoons capers, drained
¼   teaspoon salt

FIRST Cook bacon in a 12-inch skillet over medium heat until crisp, about 3 minutes. Add onion, garlic and peppers; sauté until soft, about 5 minutes. Stir in artichoke hearts, wine, stock, thyme and oregano. Bring to a simmer and cook for 10 minutes.

NEXT While sauce cooks, whisk flour and 2 tablespoons water in a small bowl until smooth. Stir into sauce and continue to cook an additional 3 minutes or until slightly thickened.

LAST Add shrimp and cook, stirring often, until pink, about 4 minutes. Remove from heat; stir in lemon zest, juice, parsley, capers and salt. Season to taste with freshly ground black pepper. Serve over Goat Cheese Grits (page 154).

Lime Grilled Chicken

This easy chicken recipe is full of vibrant flavors. If you don't care for chicken thighs, use skin-on chicken breasts instead. Serve with an avocado and tomato salad plus black beans and rice, and it might just become your new favorite weeknight meal.

PREP TIME 15 minutes
COOK TIME 10 minutes
YIELDS 6 servings

8   chicken thighs, skin on
2½ tablespoons olive oil, divided
2   garlic cloves, minced
½   teaspoon ground cumin
½   cup fresh lime juice (from about 7 limes)

FIRST Preheat grill to medium-high heat, about 350° to 400°F. Season chicken generously with kosher salt and freshly ground black pepper. Brush chicken lightly with 1 tablespoon oil and grill, with lid closed, about 5 minutes per side or until meat thermometer inserted in thickest part registers 165°F.

NEXT While chicken cooks, heat remaining oil in a small skillet over medium heat. Add garlic and cumin and cook until fragrant, about 30 seconds. In a large glass baking dish, combine garlic mixture and lime juice; season with freshly ground black pepper.

LAST Place cooked chicken thighs in glass dish, turning to coat chicken with lime mixture. Tent with foil and let rest 10 minutes before serving.

Honey Soy-Glazed Quail

My dad is an avid quail hunter, and our farm in South Georgia has provided
many wonderful memories and quail hunts for our family. After a long day on the wagon and
horses, it's fun to sit down to a quail supper and share a bottle of wine, good stories and
great company. This recipe combines two of my favorite ingredients, soy and ginger,
to create a beautiful, lustrous glaze for these special birds.

PREP TIME 10 minutes plus 1 hour
 marinating time
COOK TIME 25 minutes
YIELDS 4 servings

8 bone-in quail
⅓ cup honey
⅓ cup soy sauce
1 tablespoon finely grated fresh ginger
4 garlic cloves, crushed
½ teaspoon Chinese five-spice powder

FIRST Wash quail and pat dry with paper towels. Using kitchen shears, cut along both sides of the backbones; discard backbones. Place quail in a glass baking dish and set aside.

NEXT In a small bowl, whisk together honey, soy, ginger, garlic and five-spice powder; season with freshly ground black pepper. Reserve 3 tablespoons glaze for basting and pour remaining glaze over quail, tossing gently to coat. Refrigerate quail for 1 hour, tossing after 30 minutes.

LAST Preheat oven to 400°F. Allow quail to sit at room temperature for 10 minutes. Place a wire cooling rack over a large rimmed baking sheet lined with foil. Arrange quail on rack, breast sides up, and brush with any marinade remaining in bottom of baking dish. Roast until thermometer inserted in thickest part of breast registers 160°F, about 20 to 25 minutes, depending on size of birds. During the last 10 minutes of cooking, brush quail with half of reserved glaze; brush with remaining half just before serving.

Grilled Ribeyes
with Rosemary Mayonnaise

As my daddy says, everything tastes better with mayonnaise.
Similar to a compound butter, homemade rosemary mayonnaise melts right over warm steaks and
makes for a mouthwatering meal. You can also try it on filets or grilled chicken.

PREP TIME 30 minutes
COOK TIME 10 minutes
YIELDS 4 servings

4 (1 ½-inch-thick) ribeye steaks
2 teaspoons kosher salt
Freshly ground black pepper
2 tablespoons Roasted Garlic-Rosemary
    Mayonnaise (page 105)

FIRST Season steaks on both sides with salt and pepper to taste; let sit at room temperature for 30 minutes. Preheat grill to medium-high heat.

NEXT Grill steaks 4 to 5 minutes per side, or until meat thermometer registers 120°F for rare or 130°F for medium-rare.

LAST Spoon 1 teaspoon mayonnaise over each warm steak. Let rest 10 minutes before serving.

Lemon-Roasted Fish

with Olives and Capers

My family eats fish more than any other protein, so I'm always thinking of new ways to prepare it. This roasted version is one of my favorites. Served over orzo and sautéed spinach, it's bright with flavor and always a hit.

PREP TIME 10 minutes
COOK TIME 30 minutes
YIELDS 4 servings

2 Meyer or regular lemons, very thinly sliced
½ tablespoon olive oil
4 (6-ounce) fillets flounder or other delicate white fish
½ cup white wine
½ cup chicken stock
3 tablespoons fresh lemon juice, divided
4 teaspoons flour
1 tablespoon capers
½ cup assorted olives
Cooked orzo and sautéed spinach to serve (see below)

FIRST Preheat oven to 425°F. Arrange lemons in a single layer in a greased 9x13-inch glass baking dish. Drizzle with olive oil and season with freshly ground black pepper. Roast in oven for 15 minutes or until lemons begin to brown around the edges.

NEXT In a small bowl, whisk wine, stock, 2 tablespoons lemon juice and flour. Arrange fish in a single layer over roasted lemons. Pour wine mixture over fish; top with capers and olives. Season fish with salt and freshly ground black pepper. Bake 12 to 15 minutes or until fish flakes easily with a fork.

LAST Drizzle fish with remaining tablespoon lemon juice. Divide fish among 4 serving plates. Top with sauce, olives and lemons from baking dish. Serve with orzo and sautéed spinach.

> **SAUTÉED SPINACH** Heat 2 cloves minced garlic and 2 teaspoons olive oil in a large skillet over medium heat. Add 5 ounces fresh spinach, salt and a splash of white wine and sauté until spinach begins to wilt, about 2 minutes.

Pecan Horseradish-Stuffed Trout

Our local market carries delicious rainbow trout from Sunburst Trout Farms, a family-owned, third-generation outfit in North Carolina. I cook trout at least once a week and this has become a favorite. For a crowd, double the stuffing and sandwich it between two sides of wild salmon.

PREP TIME 15 minutes
COOK TIME 12 minutes
YIELDS 4 servings

2½ cups fresh whole-wheat breadcrumbs, from about 2 standard slices bread
½   cup pecans, toasted and finely ground
¼   cup chopped flat-leaf parsley
Zest of 1 lemon
2   tablespoons prepared horseradish
1   tablespoon finely chopped fresh chives
2   teaspoons fresh lemon juice
1   egg, lightly beaten
½   teaspoon salt
½   teaspoon freshly ground black pepper
4   (6-ounce) trout fillets, boned, skin left intact
Lemon wedges for serving

Special equipment: kitchen string (optional)

FIRST Preheat oven to 400°F. In a large bowl, combine breadcrumbs, pecans, parsley, zest, horseradish, chives and lemon juice. Fold in egg and season with salt and freshly ground black pepper.

NEXT Rinse trout and pat dry. Place two fillets, skin sides down, on a baking sheet lined with parchment. Spread pecan mixture evenly over fish and press remaining fillets on top, skin sides up. Secure with string, if desired.

LAST Bake 12 minutes or until fish flakes easily with fork. Cut stuffed fillets in half to yield 4 pieces. Serve with lemon wedges.

Doves in Red Wine

I clearly remember my first dove hunt as a little girl. Too young to shoot,
I was the token retriever for my dad, running as fast as I could alongside the Labs and
Boykin spaniels. These days I'm better at cooking doves than fetching them, and this has become
my favorite method by far. The small birds stay tender and juicy and don't taste gamy at all.
I serve them over rice to soak up all the good red wine sauce.

PREP TIME 15 minutes
COOK TIME 50 minutes
YIELDS 4 servings

2   tablespoons butter
1   medium onion, chopped (about 1 ½ cups)
18 doves, patted dry
2   tablespoons chopped flat-leaf parsley
1   tablespoon Worcestershire sauce
½   teaspoon dried thyme
½   cup red wine
1   cup beef stock
1   tablespoon all-purpose flour

FIRST Melt butter in a Dutch oven over medium-high heat. Add onion and sauté until tender, about 5 minutes. Season doves with salt and freshly ground black pepper and place breast sides down in Dutch oven, pushing onion aside so that meat touches bottom of pan. Brown doves on both sides, about 3 minutes per side.

NEXT Add parsley, Worcestershire sauce and thyme. Add wine and simmer until reduced by half, about 5 minutes. Add stock; cover and reduce heat to low. Simmer for 30 minutes. In a small bowl, whisk flour with 1 tablespoon water. Using tongs, transfer doves to a plate and tent loosely with foil to keep warm. Increase heat to medium-high and whisk flour mixture into pot. Cook until sauce thickens slightly, about 2 minutes.

LAST Return doves to pot and ladle sauce over to coat. Season to taste with freshly ground black pepper. Serve over rice, topping with sauce.

Rosemary-Garlic
Grilled Venison Backstrap

My brother loves deer hunting, so venison was never in short supply growing up.
I don't mean to brag, but this might be the only grilled venison recipe you will ever need — it
is amazing. If you prefer, try it with elk or other large game. I strongly recommend brining
if you have the extra 30 minutes; it makes a world of difference.

PREP TIME 10 minutes plus 30 minutes
brining time
COOK TIME 15 minutes
YIELDS 6 to 8 servings

Brine (optional)

½ cup sugar
½ cup kosher salt
6 cups water

Sauce

¼ cup Dijon mustard
¼ cup olive oil
2 tablespoons red wine vinegar
1 tablespoon chopped fresh rosemary
3 cloves garlic, chopped
1 teaspoon salt

1 trimmed venison backstrap (tenderloin),
about 2 pounds

FIRST In a large saucepan over high heat, dissolve sugar and salt in 6 cups water. Let cool slightly. Place backstrap in a large bowl and pour brine over. Top with two scoops ice to keep cool. Brine for 30 minutes, but no longer. Remove venison from brine, pat dry and set aside.

NEXT Preheat grill to medium-high heat, about 450°F, and clean grates if needed. In a medium bowl, combine mustard, oil, vinegar, rosemary, garlic and salt; season generously with freshly ground black pepper. Brush two-thirds of sauce over venison, reserving remaining for basting.

LAST Grill venison on an open grill on one side for 6 to 8 minutes, basting occasionally, without turning. When venison is nicely seared with good grill marks, flip and grill on other side until meat thermometer inserted in thickest part registers 130° to 135°F for medium rare, about 5 to 8 more minutes. Remove from grill, place on cutting board and let rest for 10 minutes before carving. Cut into 1-inch slices and serve.

Maple Pecan-Glazed Chicken

We love roasted chicken in our household, and there are a million ways to make it. This is one of our favorites – my husband savors the extra-crisp skin from the sweet pecan glaze. It cooks beautifully in the oven, but it's also excellent grilled and served with roasted sweet potatoes.

PREP TIME 20 minutes
COOK TIME 45 minutes
YIELDS 4 servings

Glaze

⅓ cup maple syrup
½ cup chopped pecans
1 tablespoon apple cider vinegar

1 (3-pound) whole chicken
2 tablespoons softened butter
1 teaspoon minced garlic
2 tablespoons olive oil

FIRST Adjust oven rack to middle position and preheat oven to 375°F. Combine syrup, pecans and vinegar in a small bowl and set aside. Rinse chicken and pat dry. Butterfly chicken by cutting down both sides of backbone with sharp kitchen shears. Place chicken breast side up; using palm of your hand, press on breastbone to flatten. Using shears, cut down centers of breast halves to divide chicken in half. Arrange chicken halves on foil-lined baking sheet coated with cooking spray or oil.

NEXT In a small bowl, combine butter and garlic. Rub under skin, making sure to layer a little extra under skin of breasts. Brush skin with oil; season generously with salt and freshly ground black pepper.

LAST Roast chicken 20 minutes. Brush with half of glaze and return to oven for 10 minutes. Brush with remaining glaze and cook until meat thermometer inserted in thickest part of breast registers 165°F and chicken is golden brown, about 15 more minutes. Let rest 10 minutes before serving.

Italian Sausage and Tomato Soup

This is one of the easiest soups you'll ever make. Served with fresh bread and a good salad, it's perfect winter comfort food. I shared it with my husband's Aunt Gay, and it has become her go-to dish for feeding a crowd — she says the men usually go back for thirds and everyone requests the recipe. I'll take that as a compliment any day.

PREP TIME 15 minutes
COOK TIME 30 minutes
YIELDS 8 to 10 servings

1½ pounds Italian turkey sausage,
   casings removed
1   medium onion, chopped
3   cloves garlic, minced
1   (8-ounce) package sliced mushrooms
1½ teaspoons dried oregano
1   teaspoon dried thyme
2   (14-ounce) cans diced tomatoes, undrained
4   cups beef stock
1   cup penne pasta, uncooked
4   cups fresh spinach or chopped fresh kale
½   cup chopped fresh basil
Freshly grated Parmesan cheese for serving

FIRST In a large pot over medium-high heat, brown sausage, onions and garlic, using spoon to break sausage into small chunks, about 4 minutes. Add mushrooms and cook an additional 3 minutes, until mushrooms are tender and sausage is fully cooked.

NEXT Drain fat from sausage mixture and stir in oregano, thyme, tomatoes and stock. Cover with lid; simmer 10 minutes. Add pasta and simmer until al dente, about 8 minutes.

LAST Just before serving, add spinach and basil; stir until wilted. Season to taste with salt and freshly ground black pepper. Ladle into bowls and top with grated Parmesan.

FROM MY KITCHEN If you make this ahead of time, leave out the pasta and add it when you reheat the soup. Otherwise, it will overcook.

Easy Barbecue
with Marinated Slaw

I love barbecue, but my schedule leaves little time for slow-cooking pork.
So I devised a shortcut version that's as tasty as the traditional method and feeds a small crowd.
My mom always makes big batches of this delicious slaw to serve with burgers when we have
picnics on family quail hunts, but it lends the perfect crunch to a pulled-pork sandwich too.

PREP TIME 20 minutes
COOK TIME 25 minutes
YIELDS 8 servings

Slaw

6   cups finely shredded cabbage or
    2 (10-ounce) bags Angel Hair coleslaw mix
½   cup finely chopped Vidalia onion
½   cup plus 2 tablespoons white vinegar
2   tablespoons sugar
1½ teaspoons salt
1   teaspoon celery seed
¼   cup canola oil

Pork

1   cup tomato sauce
¼   cup brown sugar
¼   cup yellow mustard
¼   cup apple cider vinegar
¼   cup finely chopped Vidalia onion
3   tablespoons Worcestershire sauce
2   (1-pound) pork tenderloins, trimmed,
    silverskin removed

FIRST To prepare slaw, place cabbage and onion in a large bowl and set aside. Heat vinegar, sugar, salt and celery seed in a small saucepan until sugar has dissolved. Drizzle sauce and oil over cabbage and toss until coated. Season to taste with freshly ground black pepper; let marinate 20 minutes before serving.

NEXT Preheat grill to 400°F. Combine tomato sauce, brown sugar, mustard, vinegar, onion and Worcestershire in a medium saucepan over medium heat. Simmer for 8 to 10 minutes, stirring often, until sauce has thickened. Place pork in a glass baking dish and drizzle ¼ cup sauce over pork, turning to coat. Grill pork for 7 to 8 minutes per side or until a meat thermometer registers 145°F. Remove pork from grill and let rest 15 minutes.

LAST Using a serrated knife, thinly slice pork or cut into 2-inch slices and shred with hands. Toss pork with desired amount of sauce. Serve over warmed buns with slaw.

FROM MY KITCHEN This slaw is even tastier when you make it a day ahead of time. It releases moisture overnight, so toss in a little extra cabbage just before serving, which soaks up some of the extra juices and boosts the crunch.

Cedar-Planked Salmon
with Honey Lime Glaze

Grilling salmon on a cedar plank has become my absolute favorite way
to prepare it. Not only is this method super-easy, but it also makes cooking fish
foolproof — no drying out, flaking or falling through the grill grates.
Plus, the sweet, smoky flavor that the cedar lends is amazing.

PREP TIME 5 minutes
COOK TIME 15 minutes
YIELDS 4 servings

2 tablespoons honey
1 tablespoon fresh lime juice
½ tablespoon Dijon mustard
½ tablespoon whole-grain mustard
1½ pounds fresh salmon, preferably wild
1 (15-inch) cedar grilling plank, soaked in water

FIRST Preheat grill to medium-low heat, about 350°F. In a small bowl, combine honey, lime juice and mustards. Season with salt and freshly ground black pepper; brush over salmon.

NEXT Place soaked plank on grill grates, close lid and heat for about 3 minutes or until a light smoke develops. Using tongs, flip plank and place salmon on it. Close lid and cook until salmon is slightly pink in center, about 12 to 15 minutes depending on thickness of fish.

LAST Carefully remove plank from grill, leaving salmon in place, and set on metal baking sheet to cool. (Salmon will continue to cook after it's removed from the grill, so you may choose to take it off a little early.) Cut into fillets and serve.

Chicken, Artichoke and Wild Rice Casserole

Casseroles were a mainstay of church suppers in my hometown, and my mom also relied on them when she had a big group to feed. So many recipes start with cream of chicken soup and a stick of butter that I rarely make them, but this one is full of flavor, good for you and always a crowd-pleaser. Brown and wild rice are heart-healthy, though they take a little longer to cook.

PREP TIME 30 minutes
COOK TIME 1 hour and 30 minutes
YIELDS 6 servings

1   cup brown and wild rice blend, uncooked (such as Rice Select or Lundberg)
2   teaspoons olive oil, plus more for coating dish
2   leeks, white and light green parts only, halved lengthwise, washed and thinly sliced
¼   teaspoon salt, plus more to taste
5   ounces baby portabella mushrooms, sliced
2   tablespoons fresh thyme, divided
2   cloves garlic, chopped
1   cup sherry (see From My Kitchen, below)
¼   cup all-purpose flour
2   cups 1 percent milk
1   cup low-sodium chicken stock
½   cup reduced-fat sour cream
½   cup freshly grated Parmesan cheese
½   cup grated Gruyère cheese
3   boneless, skinless chicken breasts (about 1 ½ pounds), cut into ½-inch pieces
1   (14-ounce) can artichoke hearts, drained and quartered
5   ounces fresh spinach, lightly steamed and drained
½   cup slivered almonds

FIRST Preheat oven to 350°F. Coat a 9x13-inch baking dish with oil and spread rice in an even layer in dish; set aside. Heat 2 teaspoons oil in a large pot or Dutch oven over medium heat. Add leeks and salt and cook, stirring occasionally, until lightly browned, about 5 minutes. Stir in mushrooms and 1 tablespoon thyme; cook until released liquid evaporates, about 6 to 8 minutes.

NEXT Add remaining thyme, garlic and sherry. Increase heat to medium-high and cook until liquid has reduced by half, about 4 minutes. Sprinkle mushroom mixture with flour, stirring to coat. Add milk and stock; cook 2 minutes or until slightly thickened. Stir in sour cream and cheeses; season to taste with salt and freshly ground black pepper.

LAST Top rice with chicken and artichoke hearts. Spread spinach leaves over and top with mushroom mixture. Sprinkle almonds evenly over top, cover with foil and bake for 30 minutes. Remove foil and continue cooking for 40 minutes. Let rest 10 minutes before serving.

> **FROM MY KITCHEN** You can find inexpensive sherry in the wine department of your grocery store or at a wine shop. Don't buy the kind in the vinegar section labeled "sherry cooking wine" — it lacks flavor and is quite strong.

Goat Cheese Grits

Stone-ground grits are the South's version of polenta.
You can serve them as a side or add other ingredients to make a hearty main dish.
Try a variety of cheeses and toppings, such as sautéed mushrooms, tomatoes and basil, or wilted greens. Fresh goat cheese is a perfect match for my Shrimp and Grits (page 129).

PREP TIME 5 minutes
COOK TIME 45 minutes
YIELDS 4 servings

2 cups low-sodium chicken stock
2 cups water
1 cup stone-ground grits, uncooked
½ teaspoon salt
Pinch baking soda
1 tablespoon butter
1 ounce fresh goat cheese

FIRST Bring stock and water to a boil in a large stockpot. Slowly whisk in grits; add salt and baking soda. Cook, uncovered, for 40 to 45 minutes or until done. Stir in butter and cheese and serve.

Low Country Boil

There is no better Southern tradition than a summer Low Country boil.
My dad would bring back loads of fresh shrimp, oysters and, sometimes, crab from
his fishing trips on the Gulf. He'd invite friends over and set up a propane cooker in
our driveway; my mom would spread newspaper over tables and set out bowls of homemade
cocktail sauce, melted butter and lemon. Everyone would snack on raw oysters until
the shrimp were cooked, then we'd all sit down and feast to our hearts' content.
What a wonderful way to celebrate summer with friends and family!

PICTURED ON PAGES 118-119

PREP TIME 25 minutes
COOK TIME 20 minutes
YIELDS 6 to 8 servings

Seasoning

1½ teaspoons smoked paprika
1½ teaspoons cayenne pepper
1½ teaspoons mustard seeds
1½ teaspoons fennel seeds

1   tablespoon olive oil
5   cloves garlic, mashed
5   bay leaves
1½ tablespoons sea salt
1½ pounds baby Yukon Gold potatoes
4   ears sweet corn, shucked, sliced into
    2-inch rounds
2   Vidalia onions, peeled and cut into wedges
1   pound smoked link sausage, cut into
    2-inch pieces
3   pounds medium fresh shrimp

To Serve

Melted butter
Lemon wedges
Fresh baguettes

FIRST Combine seasoning mixture in a small bowl and set aside.

NEXT Heat oil in an extra-large stockpot set over medium heat. Add garlic and stir until fragrant, about 30 seconds. Add seasoning mixture, 4 to 5 quarts water, bay leaves, salt and potatoes. Bring to a boil and cook 5 minutes. Add corn, onions and sausage and cook until potatoes are tender, about 10 more minutes. Stir in shrimp and cook until they turn pink, about 3 minutes. Drain immediately. Spread out on a table covered with newspaper or paper bags.

LAST Serve with melted butter, lemon wedges and fresh baguettes.

Sides

::

- Smoked Cheddar Popovers
- Joanie's Cornbread
- Cilantro-Lime Rice
- Butterbeans
- Roasted Cauliflower
- Balsamic Roasted Brussels Sprouts
- Cane Syrup-Glazed Carrots
- Roasted Cabbage
- Roasted Sweet Potatoes and Pears
- Squash Casserole
- Grilled Okra
- Skillet Creamed Corn
- Wilted Kale
- Warm Potatoes and Spinach
- Lady Pea and Tomato Salad (pictured)

::

Smoked Cheddar Popovers

Serve these little pieces of heaven to your friends, and
they'll think you have slaved in the kitchen for hours. They're delicious straight out of
the oven — my kids can't seem to get enough of them.

PREP TIME 15 minutes
COOK TIME 45 minutes
YIELDS 8 servings

3 eggs
1¼ cups whole or 2 percent milk
1¼ cups all-purpose flour, sifted
¼ teaspoon salt
3 tablespoons butter, melted,
     plus more for greasing pan
¾ cup shredded smoked cheddar cheese

FIRST Adjust oven rack to middle position and preheat
oven to 400°F. Butter 8 muffin or popover cups and set
aside. Beat eggs in a large mixing bowl, then gradually pour
in milk, whisking until mixed well.

NEXT Gently spoon flour into egg mixture, a little at a time,
whisking after each addition until well blended and very few
lumps remain. Whisk in salt and butter; fold in cheddar.

LAST Ladle batter into each cup, filling about ¾ full. Bake
until puffy and golden brown, about 40 to 45 minutes. Let
cool slightly. Loosen each popover with a knife to remove
from pan. Serve warm with butter, if desired.

Joanie's Cornbread
with Okra and Vidalias

I had to get a hands-on lesson to learn my mama's cornbread recipe — as with her biscuits, she never measures. I love her version because it's not too sweet and the buttermilk adds a little tang, but I also love adding extra ingredients to mine, especially okra. Get creative and stir in crumbled bacon, fresh corn kernels, chopped jalapenos or any other tidbits you want.

PREP TIME 10 minutes
COOK TIME 40 minutes
YIELDS 8 servings

¼ cup canola oil
1½ cups white cornmeal
¼ cup plus 2 tablespoons all-purpose flour
2 tablespoons baking powder
2 tablespoons sugar
1 teaspoon kosher salt
8 ounces light or regular sour cream
1 egg, lightly beaten
1¾ cups buttermilk
1½ cups okra, cut into ½-inch slices
1 cup chopped Vidalia onion

Special equipment: 10-inch cast-iron skillet
    (I prefer Lodge brand)

FIRST Preheat oven to 425°F. Pour oil into skillet and place in oven to heat.

NEXT Meanwhile, in a large bowl, combine cornmeal, flour, baking powder, sugar and salt. Add sour cream, egg and buttermilk; whisk until smooth. Fold in okra and onions. Remove skillet from oven and carefully pour hot oil into batter. Fold in oil with a wooden spoon and pour batter into hot skillet.

LAST Bake until cornbread is golden brown and knife inserted in center comes out clean, about 35 to 40 minutes.

Cilantro-Lime Rice

With fresh, bright flavors, this rice complements so many dishes and takes almost no time to prepare. Serve it with roasted chicken for a warm, comforting meal with a bit of a twist.

PREP TIME 10 minutes
COOK TIME 15 minutes
YIELDS 4 servings

1   cup jasmine rice, uncooked
2   cups water
1   teaspoon salt
⅔   cup cilantro leaves, loosely packed
2   scallions, white and light green parts, chopped (about ¼ cup)
2   tablespoons fresh lime juice
1   tablespoon olive oil

FIRST Place rice in a fine-mesh strainer and rinse under cold water; set aside. Bring 2 cups water to a boil in a large saucepan. Add salt and rice. Reduce heat to low; cover and cook until done, about 15 minutes.

NEXT While rice is cooking, combine cilantro, scallions, lime juice and olive oil in a food processor. Puree until smooth. Season with salt and freshly ground black pepper to taste.

LAST Gently toss rice with cilantro mixture, fluff with fork and serve.

Butterbeans

with Lemon, Mint and Parmesan

When spring comes around, I head straight to the market for fava beans and savor them bite by bite with fresh mint and lemon. I tried the same approach with butterbeans and fell in love. This dish complements almost any warm-season meal. If you don't have butterbeans, fresh or frozen baby lima beans work too.

PREP TIME 15 minutes
COOK TIME 15 minutes
YIELDS 8 servings

1 quart low-sodium chicken stock
24 ounces butterbeans or baby lima beans
2 teaspoons salt
Zest of ½ lemon
¼ cup fresh lemon juice
2 tablespoons olive oil, plus more for serving
½ cup fresh mint leaves
1 ounce Parmesan cheese

FIRST In a 2-quart saucepan, bring stock, 4 cups water, butterbeans and salt to a boil. Reduce heat; simmer 10 minutes or until tender. Drain and set aside to cool.

LAST Place beans in a large bowl and toss with lemon zest, juice, olive oil and fresh mint. Season to taste with salt and freshly ground black pepper. Spread butterbeans on a serving platter and drizzle with additional olive oil. Using a vegetable peeler, shave Parmesan into curls and scatter over beans. Serve at room temperature or slightly chilled.

Roasted Cauliflower
with Prosciutto and Arugula

When I was growing up, cauliflower hardly ever appeared on my family's table.
Ever since my husband and I realized how easy it is to grow, it's been a staple of
our autumn meals, and we often roast it for a wonderfully nutty flavor.
Pair this warm salad with a grilled steak for a complete and delicious supper.

PREP TIME 15 minutes
COOK TIME 30 minutes
YIELDS 4 servings

1   large head cauliflower (2 pounds),
    cut into 2-inch florets
3   tablespoons olive oil, divided
½   teaspoon kosher salt
1   ounce prosciutto (about 3 slices),
    torn into 3-inch pieces
2   tablespoons sherry vinegar
1   teaspoon Dijon mustard
2   handfuls arugula or spinach
Parmesan cheese for serving
½   cup pomegranate seeds (optional)

FIRST Preheat oven to 450°F. Place rimmed baking sheet in oven to heat for 5 minutes. In a large bowl, toss cauliflower with 2 tablespoons olive oil and salt.

NEXT Carefully coat hot baking sheet with oil or cooking spray. Arrange cauliflower on sheet and roast 15 minutes. Toss; sprinkle with prosciutto pieces. Continue cooking for 10 to 15 minutes or until cauliflower is browned and crisp-tender.

LAST Meanwhile, in a small bowl, combine 1 tablespoon olive oil, vinegar and mustard. Place arugula in a large mixing bowl; toss with hot cauliflower and vinegar mixture. Season to taste with additional salt and freshly ground black pepper. Arrange salad on a platter; top with Parmesan and pomegranate seeds, if using.

Balsamic Roasted Brussels Sprouts

When my husband says, "This is my favorite recipe," I know it's a keeper.
I enjoyed this dish at a restaurant in Charleston, South Carolina, and recreated it at home.
Hands down, these are the best Brussels sprouts I have ever had.

PREP TIME 15 minutes
COOK TIME 25 minutes
YIELDS 6 servings

2   pounds Brussels sprouts
2   strips bacon, diced
1   tablespoon olive oil
12 ounces prunes, cut in half (about ⅔ cup)
2   tablespoons balsamic vinegar

FIRST Preheat oven to 425°F. Using a sharp knife, trim stem ends of Brussels sprouts. Peel off outer leaves and discard. Cut sprouts in half lengthwise, or, if large, cut into quarters.

LAST Divide sprouts between two greased baking sheets and toss with bacon, oil and prunes. Season with salt and turn cut sides down. Roast, without turning, 20 minutes or until bottom sides are golden brown and tops are lightly charred. Toss with vinegar and season to taste with freshly ground black pepper.

Cane Syrup-Glazed Carrots

Every Thanksgiving, my family makes a large batch of cane syrup.
It's an all-day event and we make the most of it: picnic lunch, Bloody Marys and
lots of friends and family. I take every opportunity to cook with the finished product — it is rich,
flavorful and so versatile. It gives these carrots a distinctive mellow taste,
but you can use pure maple syrup if that's all you have.

PREP TIME 5 minutes
COOK TIME 7 minutes
YIELDS 4 servings

1 pound small carrots, cut in half lengthwise
½ cup chicken stock
2 teaspoons sugar
½ teaspoon salt
2 tablespoons pure cane syrup
½ tablespoon butter
2 teaspoons lemon juice

FIRST Heat carrots, stock, sugar and salt in a 12-inch skillet over medium-high heat. Bring to a simmer; cover and reduce heat to medium. Cook, stirring occasionally, about 3 minutes or until carrots are almost tender.

LAST Remove lid, increase heat to high and cook, constantly stirring, until liquid is reduced to about 2 tablespoons, about 2 minutes. Stir in syrup and butter. Continue cooking, tossing to coat, for about 1 to 2 minutes or until carrots are tender. Stir in lemon juice and season with freshly ground black pepper.

Roasted Cabbage

with Lime and Cayenne

Growing up, we ate cabbage one of two ways: steamed with a pat of butter or
in my mom's coleslaw. As I got older and started cooking on my own,
I realized how underrated cabbage really is. Roasting makes it tender but also gives it
a slight crunch. You can top the cabbage with lime and cayenne for a little kick,
or try a splash of sherry vinegar and Parmesan cheese curls.

PREP TIME 10 minutes
COOK TIME 30 minutes
YIELDS 6 servings

1   medium head green cabbage
2   tablespoons olive oil
Juice of 1 lime
Cayenne pepper to taste

FIRST Preheat oven to 450°F. Cut cabbage in half and
then into quarters through the core. Cut each quarter into
1½-inch wedges. Arrange wedges in single layers on rimmed
baking sheets lined with parchment.

NEXT Sprinkle cabbage with salt and freshly ground black
pepper; brush with olive oil. Roast until cabbage is tender and
edges are browned, about 25 to 30 minutes.

LAST Squeeze lime over cabbage and sprinkle with cayenne
to taste.

Roasted Sweet Potatoes and Pears

This side dish will quickly become a regular on your table. I often double
the recipe in hopes of having leftovers for the next day, but it always disappears
the first time around. I'm partially to blame (I usually go back for thirds),
and my children also devour every bite on their plates.

PREP TIME 15 minutes
COOK TIME 40 minutes
YIELDS 6 servings

2   pounds sweet potatoes, cubed
1½ tablespoons extra-virgin coconut oil
2   teaspoons brown sugar
¾   teaspoon salt
¼   teaspoon nutmeg
2   pears
2   teaspoons lemon juice
3   tablespoons dried cranberries, rehydrated
    in hot water and drained
¼   cup pecan halves, roughly chopped
1   tablespoon balsamic vinegar

FIRST Preheat oven to 400°F. Place potatoes in a large bowl and set aside. Heat oil in a small skillet over medium heat. Drizzle oil over potatoes; toss with sugar, salt and nutmeg. Arrange potatoes in single layers on two large rimmed baking sheets coated with cooking spray. Roast 20 minutes or until undersides are lightly browned.

NEXT While potatoes are baking, cut pears into 1-inch cubes and toss with lemon juice. Remove potatoes from oven; add pears, cranberries and pecans. Toss gently and spread into single layers. Return to oven and roast for an additional 15 to 20 minutes or until potatoes are soft and caramelized.

LAST Drizzle with balsamic vinegar to serve.

Squash Casserole

Although this is a staple of our Thanksgiving menu, I crave it most in the summer months when squash is at its peak. Unlike most versions, this one starts with raw squash instead of cooked — it has a little more crunch and texture that way.

PREP TIME 15 minutes
COOK TIME 55 minutes
YIELDS 8 to 10 servings

1   tablespoon butter
½   medium onion, chopped
1   clove garlic, minced
2   pounds yellow squash, sliced
1   cup fresh whole-wheat breadcrumbs, divided
½   cup Parmesan cheese, divided
¼   cup cheddar cheese
8   ounces light sour cream
1   (5-ounce) can sliced water chestnuts
¼   cup chopped fresh parsley
1½ teaspoons dried thyme or
     3 teaspoons fresh, divided
1   teaspoon salt

FIRST Preheat oven to 350°F. Heat butter in medium skillet over medium heat. Add onion and garlic; sauté until tender, about 5 minutes. Place sliced squash in a large bowl and add onion mixture, ½ cup breadcrumbs, ¼ cup Parmesan, cheddar, sour cream, water chestnuts, parsley, 1 teaspoon thyme and salt. Mix well. Season to taste with freshly ground black pepper.

NEXT Spread squash mixture in a well-greased 8x10-inch glass baking dish. Cover with foil and bake for 20 minutes. Meanwhile, in a small bowl, combine remaining ½ cup breadcrumbs, ½ teaspoon thyme and ¼ cup Parmesan.

LAST Remove foil and sprinkle casserole with breadcrumb mixture. Continue baking until bubbly and topping is golden brown, 30 to 35 minutes.

Grilled Okra

with Yogurt Dipping Sauce

This recipe is the result of an overflowing garden of okra that my husband and I planted.
I love okra cooked just about any way — fried, roasted, boiled — but I think
grilled is my new favorite. Dunk the charred, crispy pods in
a yogurt dipping sauce for a cool touch on summer nights.

PREP TIME 15 minutes
COOK TIME 8 minutes
YIELDS 4 servings

Yogurt Sauce

1   cup low-fat Greek yogurt
1   tablespoon fresh lemon juice
½   teaspoon ground cumin
½   teaspoon salt
1   tablespoon fresh mint leaves, chopped

Okra

1½ pounds fresh okra
1   tablespoon olive oil
½   teaspoon ground cumin
¼   teaspoon ground coriander
¾   teaspoon salt
Canola oil for grilling

FIRST Preheat grill to medium heat, about 350°F. Combine yogurt, lemon juice, cumin, salt and mint in a medium bowl; set aside.

NEXT In a large bowl, toss okra with olive oil to coat. Add cumin, coriander and salt; toss gently with hands. Using tongs, dip a balled-up paper towel in canola oil and rub over hot grill grates to coat. Grill okra 3 to 4 minutes per side until lightly charred and tender.

LAST Remove okra from grill and serve on a platter with yogurt sauce for dipping.

Skillet Creamed Corn

My dad and his good friend Mr. Buster planted a "small" garden one summer for their
two families. It quickly grew into a couple of acres of Silver Queen corn, which led to me and
Mr. Buster's daughter selling the excess off the back of a Chevy pickup in downtown Reynolds.
That wasn't exactly my ideal way to spend the summer at age 13, but it sure made me appreciate
my mom's creamed corn every Sunday. I adore this quick version of her recipe;
be sure to use only fresh, super-sweet summer corn.

PREP TIME 20 minutes
COOK TIME 9 minutes
YIELDS 6 servings

6   ears corn, husks and silk removed
½   tablespoon butter or olive oil,
    plus more for finishing
½   teaspoon kosher salt
½   cup milk

FIRST Set corn over a shallow bowl and, using a sharp,
serrated knife, cut kernels from cob. Transfer kernels to food
processor; pulse until well blended and almost smooth.

LAST Heat butter or oil in a 12-inch skillet over medium heat.
Add corn and salt and cook, stirring often, about 8 minutes.
If corn is too thick, stir in milk as needed. Sprinkle with freshly
ground black pepper, drizzle with olive oil or top with butter,
and serve.

Wilted Kale
with Pickled Onions

Even if you are not a greens fan, you will be surprised at how delicious these are.
The trick is not to cook them to death; a light sauté until they are tender and a dash of vinegar
to finish them are all you need for a hearty, healthy side dish. Look for ricotta salata, a sheep's
milk cheese, in the specialty cheese section of your local market, or substitute pecorino.

PREP TIME 15 minutes
COOK TIME 15 minutes
YIELDS 4 servings

Pickled Onions

½ medium red onion, thinly sliced
½ cup apple cider vinegar
½ teaspoon salt
½ teaspoon sugar

Kale

1½ tablespoons olive oil
1 large shallot, peeled and thinly sliced
2 bunches kale, stems and center ribs
   removed (about 10 cups)
½ cup chicken stock
1½ tablespoons sherry vinegar
2 to 3 ounces ricotta salata cheese, grated

FIRST Place onion in a small bowl and stir in vinegar, salt and sugar; set aside.

LAST Heat oil in a large stockpot over medium-high heat. Sauté shallots until soft, about 3 minutes. Add kale and cook, turning with tongs, until wilted and bright green, about 2 minutes. Add stock; cover and cook until just tender, 5 to 8 minutes. Toss greens with vinegar and arrange on a large platter. Drain pickled onions and scatter on top of kale. Finish with ricotta salata.

Warm Potatoes and Spinach

with Mustard Vinaigrette

This is one of my go-to side dishes when cooking for friends and family.
I usually add extra spinach and serve it with grilled fish or steak for an easy yet delicious supper.
Yukon Gold and fingerling potatoes have a dense, creamy texture and
are perfect for roasting — their flavor is hard to beat.

PREP TIME 15 minutes
COOK TIME 30 minutes
Yields 8 servings

3   pounds baby fingerling or small Yukon Gold
    potatoes, 1 to 2 inches in diameter
1   medium red onion, cut in half and thinly sliced
2   tablespoons olive oil, plus more for
    greasing pans
2   large handfuls fresh spinach (about 4 cups)

Dressing
2   tablespoons whole-grain mustard
2   tablespoons apple cider vinegar
4   teaspoons olive oil
2   teaspoons Dijon mustard

FIRST Preheat oven to 425°F. If potatoes are larger than
1½ inches in diameter, cut in half. Grease two large rimmed
baking sheets with oil and divide potatoes and onions between
them. Toss 1 tablespoon oil with each and season to taste with
salt and freshly ground black pepper. Spread potatoes into a
single layer and roast 25 to 30 minutes or until skin is golden
and flesh is fork-tender, tossing occasionally.

NEXT While potatoes are cooking, whisk together whole-
grain mustard, vinegar, olive oil and Dijon in a small bowl.
Set aside.

LAST Place spinach in a large bowl and add hot potato
mixture. Toss with dressing and season with additional salt
and pepper if needed. Serve immediately.

Lady Pea and Tomato Salad

I can't even begin to count how many peas I shelled as a kid, sitting on the back porch with my mom and my Grandmama Peggy. My attention span was only so long; I'd usually end up dumping my share of peas in my grandmother's bowl so I could run off to play in the woods.

PICTURED ON PAGES 156-157

PREP TIME 15 minutes
COOK TIME 10 minutes
YIELDS 8 servings

Dressing

1½ tablespoons apple cider vinegar
1 tablespoon fresh lemon juice
½ teaspoon sugar
1 small clove garlic, minced
3 tablespoons olive oil

Salad

1½ pounds fresh, shelled lady peas or
     pinkeye peas
2 teaspoons kosher salt
1 cup thinly sliced cucumber
½ small Vidalia onion, cut in half and
     thinly sliced
Small handful fresh basil or mint leaves, chopped
1½ cups assorted small tomatoes, sliced

FIRST In a small bowl, whisk together vinegar, lemon juice, sugar, garlic and olive oil. Season to taste with salt and freshly ground black pepper; set aside.

NEXT Bring 8 cups water to a boil in a large stockpot. Add peas and salt. Simmer peas until tender, about 10 minutes. Drain and let cool.

LAST Place peas in a large mixing bowl and toss with dressing, cucumber, onions and basil or mint. Gently fold in tomatoes and arrange on a large platter. Season with freshly ground black pepper and additional salt if needed. Serve at room temperature or slightly chilled.

> **FROM MY KITCHEN** If time allows, leave the salad to marinate in refrigerator for at least an hour before you add the tomatoes and basil. The oil in the dressing will solidify in the fridge, so let the dish sit at room temperature for a few minutes before serving.

Desserts

- Lemon Buttermilk Bundt Cake
- Chocolate Chip Oatmeal Creme Pies
- Bourbon-Roasted Banana Parfaits
- Homemade Hot Chocolate
- Peter's Decadent Brownies
- Strawberry Shortcake
- Pecan Sandies
- Coconut Date Balls
- Eppie's Gingerbread
- Fresh Peach and Vanilla Cream Pie
- Creamsicle Floats
- Mama Chess' Caramel Cake
- Butterscotch Pie
- Pecan Pastry Crust
- Caramel Icing

Lemon Buttermilk Bundt Cake

Bundt cakes are such a tradition in the South. My childhood church, Reynolds United Methodist, often hosted lunch after Sunday morning services, and the dessert table was worth the long wait. I can remember the long line of sweets like it was yesterday: towering layer cakes, lemon squares and bundt cakes of every shape and color.

PREP TIME 30 minutes
COOK TIME 50 minutes
YIELDS 10 servings

Cake

3 tablespoons fresh lemon juice
2 tablespoons finely grated lemon zest
3¼ cups all-purpose flour
1 teaspoon baking powder
½ teaspoon baking soda
1 teaspoon salt
3 large eggs plus 1 egg yolk, room temperature
¾ cup buttermilk
1 teaspoon vanilla extract
2¼ sticks butter, softened (see From My Kitchen, below)
2 cups sugar
Cooking spray with flour (such as Baker's Joy)

Glaze

1½ cups powdered sugar
2 tablespoons fresh lemon juice
2 tablespoons buttermilk

FIRST Adjust oven rack to lower middle position and preheat oven to 350°F. Place lemon juice and zest in a small bowl and set aside. Whisk together flour, baking powder, soda and salt in a large bowl and set aside. Whisk together eggs and yolk in a small bowl.

NEXT Combine lemon juice mixture, buttermilk and vanilla in a small mixing bowl and set aside. Using a stand mixer with paddle attachment, beat butter and sugar on medium-high speed until fluffy, about 3 minutes. Reduce speed to medium and add half of eggs; mix until incorporated, stopping to scrape sides and bottom of bowl with rubber spatula. Repeat with remaining eggs. Reduce speed to low; add ⅓ of flour mixture and half of buttermilk, beating after each addition until smooth. Repeat with remaining flour mixture and buttermilk, ending with flour mixture and scraping bowl as needed. Give batter a final stir by hand and pour into a 12-cup bundt pan coated well with cooking spray.

LAST Bake until cake is lightly browned and skewer inserted in center comes out clean, about 45 to 50 minutes. Allow cake to cool in pan on wire rack for 10 minutes, then turn out of pan onto rack. While cake is baking, prepare glaze: Whisk sugar, lemon juice and buttermilk in a small bowl until smooth. Drizzle half of glaze over warm cake. Let stand 30 minutes; repeat with remaining glaze. Allow cake to cool to room temperature before serving.

> **FROM MY KITCHEN** Softened butter should have an internal temperature of 60°F for the perfect cake. Use a meat thermometer to gauge when it's just right.

Chocolate Chip Oatmeal Creme Pies

My friend Susanna always had Little Debbie oatmeal creme pies in her
lunchbox at school, and I was always jealous. Now I love making them for my own kids,
and I just had to add a little chocolate — it makes everything taste better!
I make the pies small since they're so sweet and indulgent.

PREP TIME 40 minutes
COOK TIME 10 minutes
YIELDS 29 creme pies

1¼ cups rolled oats
¾ cup all-purpose flour
1 teaspoon cinnamon
½ teaspoon baking powder
½ teaspoon salt
½ cup (1 stick) butter, softened
¾ cup sugar
2 tablespoons molasses
1 egg
1 teaspoon vanilla
1 cup semisweet chocolate chips
1½ cups marshmallow creme

FIRST Preheat oven to 350°F. Line two baking sheets
with parchment paper and set aside.

NEXT In a large bowl, combine oats, flour, cinnamon,
baking powder and salt; set aside. Using a handheld or
stand mixer, beat butter and sugar on medium-high speed
until fluffy, about 3 minutes. Add molasses, egg and vanilla
and beat until smooth. Reduce speed to low; add flour
mixture ¼ cup at a time and beat until combined. Stir in
chocolate chips. Spoon dough by heaping teaspoonfuls
onto prepared baking sheets, spacing 3 inches apart.
Bake 8 to 10 minutes or until edges begin to brown. Cool
for 4 minutes on baking sheets, then transfer to wire rack
to cool completely.

LAST Spread 2 teaspoons marshmallow creme onto
underside of one cookie. Top with another cookie; press
together lightly to form a sandwich.

Bourbon-Roasted Banana Parfaits

When I was a child, my family would drive to Macon, Georgia, for an occasional fancy dinner at Natalia's Restaurant. My mom always ordered Bananas Foster, her favorite dessert. These parfaits are very similar, but a little more hands-off. Roasting the bananas and then layering them in make-ahead parfaits is a great approach for parties, or perfect as an everyday treat to have on hand.

PREP TIME 25 minutes
COOK TIME 35 minutes
YIELDS 6 servings

6   almost-ripe bananas, peeled, sliced
    ½-inch thick
¼   cup light brown sugar
1½ tablespoons unsalted butter, cut into
    small pieces
2   tablespoons bourbon
30 crushed vanilla wafers, plus 6 crushed
    vanilla wafers for topping
1½ quarts vanilla ice cream or frozen yogurt

Special equipment: 6 (½-pint) glass jars or
    freezer-safe glasses

FIRST Preheat oven to 400°F. Coat a 9x13-inch glass baking dish with cooking spray or butter. Place banana slices in dish and gently toss with brown sugar. Spread evenly across dish; top with pieces of butter. Cover with foil and bake 15 minutes. Remove foil and continue baking, stirring occasionally, for an additional 20 minutes, until the bananas are soft and browned. Remove from oven, stir in bourbon and set aside to cool.

NEXT Layer 1 tablespoon each vanilla wafers, ice cream and bananas into jars or glasses. Repeat layers, ending with bananas. Top each jar with an additional layer of ice cream and seal to edges so that you have 2 layers of wafers and bananas and 3 layers of ice cream. Cover with plastic wrap and freeze until ready to serve.

LAST Just before serving, garnish with crushed vanilla wafers.

Homemade Hot Chocolate

When I host dinner parties during the cooler months, I often serve warm, homemade hot chocolate for dessert. It's a good excuse to pull out the fine china cups that rarely get used, and it satisfies everyone's sweet tooth without being too filling. Around the holidays, you can stir in a little peppermint extract and top with fresh whipped cream for a festive spin. Dessert has never been so easy!

PREP TIME 5 minutes
COOK TIME 5 minutes
YIELDS 4 servings

1½ cups 2 percent milk
1   cup half-and-half
2   tablespoons sugar
4   ounces good-quality bittersweet chocolate, roughly chopped
¼   teaspoon peppermint extract (optional)
Whipped cream to serve (optional)

FIRST Heat milk, half-and-half and sugar in a large saucepan over medium-high heat. Bring to a boil, remove from heat and whisk in chocolate until melted and smooth. Stir in peppermint extract, if desired.

LAST Divide hot chocolate among 4 demitasses or teacups. Top with whipped cream, if desired.

Peter's Decadent Brownies

Our family friend Peter is an avid outdoorsman, a Southern gentleman and an incredible cook.
He usually arrives at our house bearing homemade goodness, whether it's Pepper Jelly (page 43)
or his sinful brownies. Slightly undercooked, they are pure heaven. I pair them with
ice cream and a warm cherry sauce to send them over the top.

PREP TIME 10 minutes
COOK TIME 40 minutes
YIELDS 16 servings

Brownies

¾ cup all-purpose flour, unsifted
½ cup cocoa powder
½ teaspoon baking powder
½ teaspoon salt
1½ sticks unsalted butter
1½ cups sugar
1½ teaspoons vanilla
3 eggs

Sauce

2 cups fresh or frozen (unthawed) pitted,
   dark cherries
¼ cup honey
¼ cup water
2 teaspoons cornstarch
1 teaspoon vanilla extract
1 teaspoon lemon juice

Vanilla ice cream or frozen yogurt to serve

FIRST Preheat oven to 325°F. Combine flour, cocoa, baking powder and salt in a medium bowl and set aside. Melt butter in a large saucepan over medium-low heat. Add sugar and vanilla; stir until sugar is dissolved. Remove from heat and gently whisk in eggs. Gradually add dry ingredients, whisking until smooth.

NEXT Pour batter into a buttered 8x8-inch baking pan. Bake about 35 to 40 minutes or until brownies are slightly undercooked. Let cool for 25 minutes.

LAST While brownies are baking and cooling, prepare sauce: In a small saucepan over medium heat, combine cherries, honey, water, cornstarch, vanilla and lemon. Bring to a boil and cook, stirring often, until mixture thickens, about 2 minutes. Set aside to cool slightly before serving. Cut brownies into 16 squares and serve with vanilla ice cream and cherry sauce.

Strawberry Shortcake

My mom's spin on traditional strawberry shortcake always garners recipe requests.
Her secret: a two-ingredient sauce that crowns plump slices of pound cake and
perfectly ripe berries. I like to make standard muffin-size cakes for my kids, but you can use
a loaf pan or extra-large muffin tins — just adjust the baking time as needed.
In summer, try this with fresh peach slices instead of strawberries.

PREP TIME 20 minutes
COOK TIME 30 minutes
YIELDS 10 to 12 servings

Cake

Cooking spray with flour (such as Baker's Joy)
1½ cups flour
¼ teaspoon baking soda
⅛ teaspoon salt
1 stick unsalted butter, softened
1 cup sugar
2 eggs, room temperature
½ cup buttermilk
½ teaspoon vanilla extract

Sauce

1 (12-ounce) can evaporated milk
¾ cup sugar

Assembly

3 cups fresh strawberries, sliced
Freshly whipped cream, sweetened, to serve

FIRST Preheat oven to 325°F. Spray a standard (not extra-large) 12-cup muffin tin with cooking spray and set aside. Combine flour, baking soda and salt in a medium bowl; set aside. Using a stand mixer with paddle attachment or a hand mixer, cream butter on medium speed, gradually adding sugar until well blended. Add eggs, one at a time, beating well after each addition and stopping as needed to scrape sides. Adjust speed to low and gradually spoon in flour mixture, alternating with buttermilk, until well incorporated. Add vanilla and mix just until blended. Spoon batter into muffin tins, filling each about ⅔ full. Batter may not fill all 12 muffin cups

NEXT Bake for 25 to 30 minutes or until toothpick inserted in center of cake comes out clean. Transfer pan to a cooling rack to cool. To make sauce, combine evaporated milk and sugar in a medium saucepan over medium-high heat. Bring to a simmer, whisking until sugar is dissolved, and cook for about 8 minutes. Set aside to cool.

LAST Once cakes have cooled, run a butter knife around outside edges to release from pan. Using a serrated knife, cut each cake in half horizontally. Place one bottom half on each plate, drizzle with sauce and top with about ⅓ cup strawberries. Top each with second half of cake and drizzle with additional sauce. Serve with freshly whipped cream.

Pecan Sandies

Our freezer was always loaded with pecans from my dad's friends who were pecan farmers. The smell of pecan sandies baking in our oven always excited my siblings and me, and now it does the same for my children. The dough keeps beautifully in the freezer for irresistible last-minute treats.

PREP TIME 15 minutes plus 3 hours chill time
COOK TIME 35 minutes
YIELDS About 45 cookies

1 cup pecans, roughly chopped
2 sticks unsalted butter, softened
⅓ cup sugar, plus more for sprinkling
½ teaspoon salt
1 teaspoon vanilla extract
2 cups all-purpose flour

FIRST Preheat oven to 350°F. Spread pecans on a baking sheet and toast, stirring occasionally, until lightly browned, about 8 minutes. Transfer pecans to a plate and let cool.

NEXT Using an electric mixer, beat butter, ⅓ cup sugar and salt on medium speed until light and fluffy. Reduce speed to low and add vanilla. Incorporate flour into mixture, one large spoonful at a time. Add pecans and mix until well incorporated.

LAST Form into 2 logs, each 2 inches around. Wrap each in plastic wrap and refrigerate at least 3 hours or overnight. Slice into ½-inch rounds and sprinkle with sugar, pressing lightly to adhere. Place on a parchment-covered baking sheet and bake at 350°F for 25 minutes or until edges are lightly browned. Let cool for 5 minutes, then transfer to cooling rack and cool completely.

Coconut Date Balls

Every Christmas when I was growing up, a family friend would drop by with
a round tin full of homemade goodies, including roasted pecans, cheese straws and
these delectable little balls of sugar. I never knew what they were made of; I just knew
I loved every bite. Today I make them for my children during the holidays,
and they always have fun helping me roll the sticky balls in coconut.

PREP TIME 30 minutes plus 1 to 2 hours
    chill time
COOK TIME 10 minutes
YIELDS About 50

1   stick unsalted butter
1   cup chopped, pitted dates
¾   cup sugar
2   eggs, beaten
¾   cup chopped pecans
1½ cups crisp rice cereal (such as Rice Krispies)
1   teaspoon vanilla extract
2   cups unsweetened flaked coconut

FIRST In a saucepan, melt butter over low heat. Stir in dates and sugar. Whisk 2 tablespoons date mixture into eggs, then slowly whisk egg mixture into saucepan. Cook over low heat for 10 minutes, whisking often, until mixture is smooth. Remove from heat; stir in pecans, cereal and vanilla.

LAST When mixture is cool enough to handle, shape into 1-inch balls with hands. Roll in coconut and place on wax paper-lined baking sheets. Refrigerate for 1 to 2 hours or until firm. Store in an airtight container in the refrigerator.

Eppie's Gingerbread
with Warm Lemon Sauce

I always love hearing stories about Eppie, a wonderful cook my mother-in-law grew up with. Her recipes have been passed down through the years, and her gingerbread is always a conversation piece. The warm lemon sauce makes a delicious accompaniment, but if you want something a little less sweet, try Greek yogurt combined with a touch of honey and orange zest.

PREP TIME 20 minutes
COOK TIME 40 minutes
YIELDS 12 servings

Gingerbread

Cooking spray with flour (such as Baker's Joy)
2¼ cups all-purpose flour
1½ teaspoons ground ginger
1 teaspoon ground cinnamon
1¾ teaspoons baking soda
½ teaspoon salt
¾ cup plus 2 tablespoons dark brown sugar
¾ cup plus 2 tablespoons canola oil
¾ cup molasses
¼ cup honey
2 eggs
Zest of ½ lemon
¾ cup boiling water

Lemon Sauce

1 cup sugar
1 cup water
½ stick unsalted butter, cut into pieces
Juice and zest of 1 large lemon
1 tablespoon all-purpose flour
Pinch of salt

FIRST Preheat oven to 350°F. Coat an 8½x11-inch square baking pan with cooking spray and set aside. Whisk together flour, spices, baking soda and salt in a large bowl. In a separate bowl, combine brown sugar, oil, molasses, honey, eggs and lemon zest. Whisk until smooth. Slowly whisk into dry ingredients until combined. Whisk in boiling water and transfer batter to greased baking dish.

NEXT Bake for 40 minutes or until cake tester inserted in center comes out clean. Place pan on wire rack to cool.

LAST To make the sauce, bring sugar and water to a boil in a medium saucepan. Reduce heat and simmer for 5 minutes; stir in butter, lemon juice and zest. Once butter has melted, whisk in flour and salt. Cook 3 minutes until slightly thickened. Cut gingerbread into squares and lightly drizzle with sauce so that it absorbs into cake.

Fresh Peach and Vanilla Cream Pie

Reynolds sits in the heart of Georgia peach country. Growing up, I could walk down
my driveway in the summertime and pick all the peaches I could eat, and every summer job
I had centered around peach season. This dessert is one of my mom's specialties and,
until I made it for this cookbook, I'd forgotten how absolutely amazing it is.
One bite takes me right back to my childhood.

PREP TIME 30 minutes plus 4 hours
    chill time
COOK TIME 10 minutes
YIELDS 16 servings

Crust

2   cups graham cracker crumbs
½   cup melted butter
⅓   cup sugar

Filling

4   egg yolks
4   cups 2 percent milk, divided
2   cups sugar
¼   cup cornstarch
1   pinch salt
1   tablespoon butter
1   teaspoon pure vanilla extract

Topping

3   large peaches, sliced
1   vitamin C tablet, crushed, or juice of ½ lemon
1   tablespoon sugar (optional)
¼   cup shredded coconut, lightly toasted

FIRST Preheat oven to 400°F. Using a fork, stir together cracker crumbs, butter and sugar. Press mixture into a 9-inch pie plate, making sure to cover bottom and sides. Bake for 10 minutes or until lightly browned; set aside to cool.

NEXT Whisk eggs and 1 cup milk in a medium mixing bowl; set aside. In a large saucepan over medium-high heat, whisk remaining 3 cups milk, sugar and cornstarch until smooth. Increase heat and bring to a low boil. Cook, stirring frequently, until mixture begins to thicken, about 8 to 10 minutes. Gently whisk in egg yolk mixture, bring to a boil and cook an additional 2 minutes, stirring constantly, until mixture thickens. Whisk in salt, butter and vanilla until smooth.

LAST Pour filling into crust (you will have some left over to enjoy with fresh fruit another time). Allow to cool for 30 minutes, then cover and refrigerate at least 4 hours or overnight. Toss sliced peaches with crushed vitamin C or lemon juice to prevent browning. Depending on sweetness of peaches, toss with a sprinkle of sugar if desired. Arrange peach slices on pie and sprinkle with coconut. Serve chilled.

Creamsicle Floats

Creamsicles were one of my favorite poolside treats as a kid. I loved that creamy center and orange outer layer. This updated version is a breeze and makes great little floats for kids or adults. They're pretty sweet, so a little goes a long way, but they're delicious!

PREP TIME 5 minutes
YIELDS 6 servings

1   quart orange sherbet
2   cups good-quality orange juice
2   cups vanilla ice cream or frozen yogurt

FIRST In a blender, puree sherbet and orange juice until smooth. Divide among 6 glasses, top each with a scoop of ice cream and serve.

Mama Chess' Caramel Cake

My maternal grandmother, Mama Chess, was famous for her old-fashioned caramel cake, and my mom has followed in her footsteps. We make two every Thanksgiving: one to enjoy immediately, one to put in the freezer for Christmas Day. The caramel icing is melt-in-your-mouth delicious — rich and thick with a matte finish and slightly gritty with sugar. Not many folks make these any more, but I encourage you to revive the tradition in your household.

PREP TIME 1 hour
COOK TIME 20 minutes
YIELDS 12 servings

3   cups sifted cake flour (such as Swansdown), plus more for preparing pans
1   teaspoon cream of tartar
½   teaspoon baking soda
2   sticks unsalted butter, softened, plus more for greasing pans
2   cups sugar
4   eggs, room temperature
1   cup milk
1   teaspoon vanilla extract
1   batch Caramel Icing (see page 215)

Special equipment:
4   (9-inch) round cake pans
Parchment paper
Icing spreader

> **FROM MY KITCHEN** If the icing gets too firm to spread before you're finished, place the bowl in a hot water bath and gently stir until the icing softens. Repeat this step as often as needed as you ice the cake.

FIRST Preheat oven to 350°F. Butter and flour the bottoms and sides of 4 (9-inch) cake pans and set aside. Using bottom of 1 cake pan as a guide, trace 4 circles on parchment paper. Cut circles out and fit inside buttered pans; butter and flour parchment. In a medium bowl, combine flour, cream of tartar and baking soda; set aside.

NEXT Using an electric mixer, cream butter and sugar until fluffy. Add eggs, one at a time, beating well after each addition. Adjust mixer speed to medium-low and gradually spoon flour mixture into butter mixture, alternating with milk, scraping down sides with a rubber spatula as needed. Add vanilla and mix until incorporated. Pour batter into prepared pans. Bake for 17 minutes or until a wooden toothpick inserted in center comes out clean. Cool cakes in pans for 10 minutes. Carefully turn cakes out of pans onto wire racks and continue to cool

LAST Prepare caramel icing (page 215) as directed. Place one cake round on a cake plate, pour enough icing over to coat top of cake and spread with icing spreader to the edges. Place second cake round on top, pour a generous amount of icing over cake and spread so that it runs down sides. Spread into an even layer on top and sides until no cake is visible. Repeat with third layer. Arrange fourth layer on top and pour on remaining icing, spreading fast but carefully so that icing does not harden. The top layer should be extra thick with icing. Smooth sides with spreader so that cake is evenly coated. If icing becomes too hard, wet hands and gently pat to smooth out any rough areas. Allow icing to sit until there is no visible sheen. Cover with plastic wrap and foil until ready to serve.

Butterscotch Pie

with Pecan Pastry Crust

Every time we visited Mama Chess, she would have a freshly baked pie ready for our arrival.
Even in her 90s, she had one heck of a sweet tooth. Maybe that's where mine comes from.

PREP TIME 20 minutes plus chill time
COOK TIME 20 minutes
YIELDS 8 servings

Pie

1   cup packed light or dark brown sugar
⅓   cup all-purpose flour
¼   teaspoon salt
1¼ cups 2 percent or whole milk
3   egg yolks, beaten
¼   cup butter, chilled
1   teaspoon vanilla
1   (9-inch) prebaked Pecan Pastry Crust
    (page 214)

Meringue

6   egg whites
¼   teaspoon cream of tartar
6   tablespoons sugar
1   teaspoon vanilla

FIRST In a medium saucepan, whisk together sugar, flour and salt. Set pan over medium heat and slowly whisk in milk. Cook mixture until it forms a thick, smooth sauce, about 8 minutes. Spoon ¼ cup warm sauce into egg yolks and whisk to combine. Slowly whisk egg mixture into saucepan and continue whisking for about 2 to 3 minutes until filling is thick and smooth. Remove from heat and stir in butter and vanilla. Pour filling into prebaked piecrust and set aside.

NEXT Adjust oven rack to middle position and preheat oven to 350°F. Beat egg whites and cream of tartar with an electric mixer on high speed until foamy. One tablespoon at a time, add sugar and beat until stiff peaks form. Add vanilla and beat until blended. Spread meringue evenly over filling, sealing to edge of crust.

LAST Bake pie until meringue is nicely browned, about 10 minutes. Let cool completely, then place in refrigerator. Chill at least 2 hours before serving.

Pecan Pastry Crust

I often replace my traditional piecrust recipe with this one. I love the nutty flavor; it reminds me of a buttery shortbread cookie laced with pecans.

PREP TIME 15 minutes plus 30 minutes
   chill time
COOK TIME 30 minutes
YIELDS 1 (9-inch) piecrust

½ cup chopped pecans
1¼ cups all-purpose flour
2 tablespoons sugar
½ cup butter, chilled
2 tablespoons cold water
1 teaspoon vanilla

FIRST In a food processor fitted with blade attachment, pulse pecans until finely chopped. Remove from processor and set aside. Add flour and sugar to processor and pulse lightly to combine. Slice chilled butter into ½-inch slices and add to processor; pulse until mixture is crumbly. Add pecans to mixture and, with motor running, pour water and vanilla through food chute. Process just until dough forms a ball. Transfer dough to a floured surface, shape into a ball and chill 30 minutes.

NEXT Roll dough between two sheets of plastic wrap to ¼-inch thickness. Transfer to a 9-inch pie plate, removing plastic wrap. Trim excess dough from edges; cover and chill for 30 minutes.

LAST Preheat oven to 350°F. Prick bottom and sides of dough with fork and line with parchment paper. Fill pie with dried beans or pie weights and bake for 20 minutes or until edges begin to brown lightly. Remove beans and paper; return crust to oven. Bake until crust is dry and evenly browned on bottom, about 8 to 10 minutes. Set aside to cool while preparing filling.

Caramel Icing

As a child I would request the largest piece of caramel cake, then eat all the icing and throw the cake part away. You can only imagine how mad this made my mom and Mama Chess after all the labor they put into baking. Unfortunately, as an adult, I have not changed.

PREP TIME 15 minutes
COOK TIME 20 minutes
YIELDS Enough icing for a 4-layer cake

5½ cups sugar, divided
½ cup light corn syrup
1 (12-ounce) can evaporated milk
2 sticks butter, sliced into tablespoons and frozen
1 teaspoon vanilla

Special equipment: candy thermometer

FIRST In a large stockpot over medium-high heat, combine 5 cups sugar, corn syrup and evaporated milk. Cook to soft-ball stage (238°F on candy thermometer). When icing has almost reached the desired temperature, heat ½ cup sugar in small cast-iron skillet over medium-high heat until sugar is completely melted and dark brown. Stir into icing and remove pot from heat.

LAST Beat mixture with a hand mixer until slightly cooled and beginning to thicken. Drop frozen butter into icing, two tablespoons at a time, until all butter is used and icing is thick; mix in vanilla. Spread icing over cake layers as directed (page 210).

FROM MY KITCHEN You can double check the soft-ball stage by dropping a small spoonful of icing into a cup of cold water to cool. Using hands, roll the icing between your fingers. It has reached soft-ball stage when it forms a pliable ball and doesn't break apart in your hands.

Breakfast

- Asparagus and Sun-Dried Tomato Frittata Cups
- Steel-Cut Oatmeal
- Goat Cheese and Chive Biscuits
- Blueberry Buttermilk Pancakes
- Raspberry Streusel Muffins
- Apple Breakfast Strata (pictured)
- Brown Sugar-Broiled Grapefruit (pictured)

Asparagus and Sun-Dried Tomato Frittata Cups

These super-easy frittata cups are a delicious addition to a breakfast or brunch spread.
If asparagus isn't in season, swap in chopped steamed broccoli.

PREP TIME 10 minutes
COOK TIME 25 minutes
YIELDS 9 individual cups

8   large eggs
¼   teaspoon salt
1   cup fresh, thin asparagus, trimmed and
    cut into ½-inch pieces
½   cup oil-packed sun-dried tomatoes,
    drained and chopped
3   tablespoons chopped fresh basil
¼   cup finely grated fresh Parmesan
¼   cup crumbled goat cheese

FIRST Preheat oven to 350°F. Beat eggs in a medium bowl; season with salt and freshly ground black pepper. Stir in asparagus, tomatoes, basil and Parmesan cheese.

NEXT Coat 9 cups of a 12-cup muffin pan with cooking spray. Ladle egg mixture into the prepared cups, sprinkle goat cheese evenly over tops and bake until set, about 25 minutes.

LAST Allow to cool for 5 minutes. Run a butter knife around edges of cups to release the frittatas. Serve warm. Store leftovers in the refrigerator and reheat in a 325°F oven.

Steel-Cut Oatmeal

with Apples and Cherries

This is by far my kids' favorite breakfast, and it beats purchased packets of oatmeal by a mile.
I make a big pot, store it in the fridge and reheat portions on the stove with a little water.
If you have no time for the baked apple topping, pile on fresh fruit and yogurt instead.

PREP TIME 10 minutes
COOK TIME 35 minutes
YIELDS 4 to 6 servings

1   tablespoon butter or coconut oil
1   cup steel-cut oats (not rolled oats)
2   cups 1 percent milk
2   cups warm water
¼   teaspoon salt
½   teaspoon cinnamon
⅛   teaspoon cardamom
1   apple, grated
½   cup dried cherries or raisins
1   teaspoon vanilla extract
¼   cup pure cane or maple syrup
Baked apples for topping (optional; see below)

FIRST Melt butter over medium heat in large saucepan. Stir in oats and toast for 2 minutes, stirring often.

NEXT Whisk in milk, water and salt. Bring to a boil; reduce heat to a low simmer and cover pan with lid. Cook 30 minutes, stirring occasionally, or until oats are tender but still have a slight bite. Stir in cinnamon, cardamom, grated apple, cherries, vanilla and syrup.

LAST Remove from heat and let cool 5 minutes. Top with baked apples, if desired, to serve.

BAKED APPLES Preheat oven to 375°F. Toss 2 thinly sliced apples with 1 tablespoon brown sugar, 1 teaspoon lemon juice and ½ teaspoon cinnamon. Spread on two baking sheets lined with parchment paper. Dot apples with 1½ tablespoons butter, cut into small pieces. Bake 20 minutes until apples are soft and edges begin to brown.

Goat Cheese and Chive Biscuits
with Smoked Salmon

Biscuits are a Saturday morning treat in our house, just as they were for me growing up. By adding creamy goat cheese and fresh chives to my mom's recipe, I've created a grown-up version that is amazing when paired with smoked salmon or trout. Serve them for brunch and they'll go like hotcakes.

PREP TIME 15 minutes
COOK TIME 15 minutes
YIELDS About 18 biscuits

2   cups self-rising soft wheat flour
    (such as White Lily)
4   tablespoons chilled butter, cut into
    small pieces, plus more for greasing pan
2   tablespoons finely chopped chives
½   teaspoon freshly cracked black pepper
1   (4-ounce) log fresh goat cheese, crumbled
1 to 1¼ cups buttermilk
6   ounces smoked salmon or trout
1   cucumber, thinly sliced

Special equipment: 2-inch biscuit cutter

FIRST Preheat oven to 450°F. Coat two baking sheets with butter. Sift flour into a large bowl. Using a pastry cutter or back of fork, cut butter into flour mixture until it resembles coarse meal. Stir in chives and pepper.

NEXT Using a fork, stir in crumbled cheese. Slowly pour enough buttermilk into flour mixture to make a sticky dough (you may not use all of the buttermilk). Lightly stir with fork until dough comes away from side of bowl. Place dough on a floured work surface, sprinkle lightly with flour and pat to a 1-inch thickness.

LAST Flour a 2-inch biscuit cutter and cut out biscuits, placing on greased baking sheet about 3 inches apart. Lightly knead remaining dough and repeat patting and cutting until all dough is used. Bake for 15 minutes or until lightly browned. Cool biscuits and cut in half horizontally using a serrated knife. Top bottom halves with smoked salmon, cucumber slices and remaining biscuit halves. Serve.

Blueberry Buttermilk Pancakes

My mom would try her best to wake me up for school every morning,
but the only thing that got me down the stairs was the anticipation of a delicious breakfast.
It was occasionally a bowl of Fruity Pebbles (which I did love), but most often
it was something homemade and delicious. Her pancakes drizzled with cane syrup
were always a warm welcome to start my day.

PREP TIME 10 minutes
COOK TIME 20 minutes
YIELDS About 18 pancakes

2   cups all-purpose flour
2   tablespoons sugar
1   teaspoon baking powder
½   teaspoon baking soda
½   teaspoon salt
2   cups buttermilk
¼   cup light or regular sour cream
2   large eggs
3   tablespoons unsalted butter, melted
1   cup fresh blueberries, washed and dried
Vegetable or coconut oil for cooking

FIRST In a medium bowl, whisk together flour, sugar, baking powder, baking soda and salt; set aside. In a separate bowl, whisk buttermilk, sour cream, eggs and butter until smooth. Make a well in the center of the flour mixture and slowly pour in wet ingredients. Whisk just until combined (lumps should still be visible). Fold in blueberries and allow batter to rest 5 minutes before cooking.

LAST Heat a 12-inch skillet over medium heat. Coat with 1 teaspoon oil and wipe down with a paper towel. Ladle ¼ cup batter to form each of 4 pancakes and cook about 2 minutes or until bubbles appear on surface and undersides of pancakes are golden brown. Flip pancakes and cook for an additional 2 minutes or until golden brown. Transfer to a wire rack set over a baking sheet and place in a 200°F oven to keep warm. Repeat with remaining batter, oiling pan as needed. Serve pancakes with pure cane or maple syrup.

Raspberry Streusel Muffins

I am not big on feeding my family breakfast muffins that resemble dessert. These represent an ideal balance: healthy, slightly sweet and incredibly delicious. I spread them with a little Greek yogurt, and my two-year-old, Genevieve, devours them in no time.

PREP TIME 20 minutes
COOK TIME 20 minutes
YIELDS 12 muffins

Muffins

¾ cup all-purpose flour
¾ cup whole-wheat flour
¼ cup toasted wheat germ
½ teaspoon baking soda
⅛ teaspoon salt
½ cup packed brown sugar
¾ cup low-fat yogurt
¼ cup low-fat milk
¼ cup melted extra-virgin coconut oil
2 eggs
½ teaspoon almond extract
1½ cups fresh raspberries

Streusel

5 tablespoons rolled oats
4 tablespoons all-purpose flour
2 tablespoons brown sugar
2 tablespoons butter, slightly softened

FIRST Preheat oven to 375°F. Line a 12-cup standard muffin pan with paper liners or spray with cooking spray that includes flour (such as Baker's Joy). Whisk together flours, wheat germ, baking soda and salt in a large bowl; set aside.

NEXT In a medium bowl, combine sugar, yogurt, milk, oil, eggs and almond extract. Make a well in the center of flour mixture and pour in egg mixture. Slowly whisk until well combined; fold in berries. Spoon batter evenly into muffin cups and set aside.

LAST Combine oats, flour, sugar and butter in a small bowl. Blend by pressing down with back of fork until mixture resembles coarse meal. Sprinkle topping evenly over unbaked muffins and bake for 20 minutes or until a wooden toothpick inserted in center comes out clean.

GENA
KNOX

Apple Breakfast Strata

Whether I'm hosting a holiday celebration or have overnight guests,
make-ahead breakfast casseroles keep mornings simple. The challenge is finding
a healthy version like this one. The heavenly aroma will wake up
even the soundest sleepers in the house.

PICTURED ON PAGES 216-217

PREP TIME 20 minutes plus overnight
  chill time
COOK TIME 45 minutes
YIELDS 6 to 8 servings

8 (1½-ounce) slices whole-wheat sandwich
    bread, cut diagonally into quarters
2 medium-firm apples, peeled, halved and
    sliced ¼ inch thick
¼ cup dried cranberries
1½ cups 1 percent milk
5 eggs
4 tablespoons brown sugar, divided
1 teaspoon vanilla extract
1 teaspoon ground cinnamon
Plain Greek yogurt and maple syrup to serve

FIRST Grease an 8x12-inch glass baking dish. Arrange half of bread slices in two long rows with points up, slightly overlapping. Distribute apple slices evenly over bread. Sprinkle with cranberries and top with remaining bread triangles.

NEXT In a medium bowl, whisk together milk, eggs, 3 tablespoons sugar, vanilla and cinnamon. Pour mixture over bread, pressing down to submerge. Sprinkle with remaining tablespoon sugar. Cover with plastic wrap and refrigerate overnight.

LAST Preheat oven to 350°F. While oven heats, remove casserole from refrigerator and let stand at room temperature. Bake for about 45 minutes or until set. Serve with yogurt and maple syrup on the side.

Brown Sugar-Broiled Grapefruit

There is no comparison to the taste of an orange or a Ruby Red grapefruit in peak season.
Christmastime usually meant boxes of fresh Florida citrus arriving at my family's door,
and broiled grapefruit was always part of our Christmas morning breakfast
along with biscuits, grits and the works.

PICTURED ON PAGES 216-217

PREP TIME 5 minutes
COOK TIME 4 minutes
YIELDS 4 servings

2   whole grapefruits
4   tablespoons brown sugar

Special equipment: Grapefruit spoons

FIRST Preheat broiler. Slice grapefruits in half crosswise. Using a paring knife, cut along the edges of each segment, but do not remove. Cut a thin slice from the bottom of each grapefruit half so that it sits upright. Arrange fruit on baking sheet and sprinkle each half with 1 tablespoon brown sugar.

LAST Broil about 4 inches from heat source for 4 minutes or until caramelized. Serve immediately with grapefruit spoons.

GENA KNOX

Acknowledgements

OVER THE PAST TWO YEARS, I have received more compliments on my last cookbook, *Southern My Way: Simple Recipes, Fresh Flavors*, than I could ever have hoped for. How rewarding it is to hear so many people talk about the stories within, their favorite recipes and their admiration of the pictures throughout the book. I never dreamed it would be so well received, nor did I dream I would be writing another one two years later.

After continual support, encouragement and pleading from friends, family and fans, here we are. I now have two children and one more on the way, so it really has taken a village and lots of hard work from everyone to make this book a reality.

My sweet family has been incredibly patient and supportive, even on the longest of photo shoots. Thank you to my mom for her inspiration and lessons throughout my childhood, and to my husband for his love and constant support. He is truly my biggest fan. Of course, I could not do any of this without the help of wonderful Ms. Velma, who keeps my children busy and occupied during my workdays.

Once again, Gill Autrey, my designer and art director, has outdone himself with his talent, patience and amazing ideas. Without Gill, who keeps me inspired every day, I never would have committed to another book.

Brian Woodcock enthusiastically joined our team as photographer, having no idea what he was getting into. He certainly did not realize how entertaining it can be to work with a four-year-old who is "all boy," to say the least. Brian's work shows off so many special places throughout the South that are a huge part of my life. His lighting and attention to detail make every dish look like you could dig right in. Thank you, Brian, for bringing our ideas to life.

I have so much trust and admiration for my editor, Lisa Frederick. She puts every story and recipe into beautiful words that bring Gill's design ideas, my recipes and Brian's photos together to create one exquisite book.

Last but not least, thank you to my sweet grandmother, Mama Chess, who passed the week this book went to print. Mama Chess, thank you for being you and for raising such an amazing daughter, my mother. I love you.

Resources and Credits

The Capra Gia Cheese Co.
(Handmade artisanal goat's milk products)
Carrollton, Georgia
770-712-8465
www.capragia.com

Pearson Farm
(Georgia peaches and pecans)
Fort Valley, Georgia
888-423-7374
www.pearsonfarm.com

Fire & Flavor Grilling Co.
(Cedar grilling planks)
Bogart, Georgia
866-728-8332
www.fireandflavor.com

Split Creek Farm
(Goat's milk cheeses, milk, fudge)
Anderson, South Carolina
864-287-3921
www.splitcreek.com

Dickey Farms
(Georgia peaches)
Musella, Georgia
1-800-PEACH-GA
www.gapeaches.com

Taylor Orchards
(Georgia peaches)
Reynolds, Georgia
478-847-4186
www.taylororchards.com

Lane Southern Orchards
(Florida citrus; Georgia peaches and pecans)
Fort Valley, Georgia
800-27-PEACH
www.lanesouthernorchards.com

Woodland Gardens
(Certified organic vegetables, fruit and cut flowers)
Athens, Georgia
706-227-1944
www.woodlandgardensorganic.com

CUTLERY & PROPS

Bloodroot Blades
(Handcrafted cutlery)
Athens, Georgia
www.bloodrootblades.com

Hawthorne House
(Wallpaper)
Athens, Georgia
706-227-3560
www.hawthornehouseinc.com

Index

Note: **Bold** page numbers indicate photographs.

Index

Index

Index

Index

Index